The Character of Meriwether Lewis

"Completely Metamorphosed" in the American West

A Humanities Essay

Book One in the Series

The American Epic

New Lenses on Lewis and Clark

Next in the Series:
The Burden of Being Clark

The most famous portrait of Meriwether Lewis was painted in 1807 by Charles Willson Peale in Philadelphia.

Published in 2000 by Marmarth Press
A Division of Empire for Liberty LLC
6015 S. Virginia Street, Suite E#458, Reno, Nevada 89502

Marmarth
Press

Marmarth Press is a trademark of Empire for Liberty LLC

Distributed by Empire Catalog
A Division of Empire for Liberty LLC

Printed in Canada

10 9 8 7 6 5 4 3 2

European Article Number: 9 781930 806016

International Standard Book Number: 1-930806-01-9
The Character of Meriwether Lewis:
"Completely Metamorphosed" in the American West

Library of Congress Catalog Card Number: 00-110663

The paper in this book meets the requirements of ANSI/NISO Z39.48-1992 (Permanence of Paper).

Please visit our website www.empirecatalog.com for additional information about Lewis and Clark and Clay S. Jenkinson.

The Character of Meriwether Lewis

"Completely Metamorphosed" in the American West

A Humanities Essay

Clay S. Jenkinson

The Marmarth Institute

To Catherine Missouri Walker Jenkinson

May she be Clark in stability
Lewis in sensitivity
Jefferson in mind
And child of the plains to the core

Contents

Illustrations

Cover art:

Captain Meriwether Lewis, 1807, by Charles B.J.F. Saint-Mémin, accession number 1971.125. © Collection of the New-York Historical Society.

Map from "Sundry Indians of the Chopunnish Nation together" on May 29, 30, and 31, 1806, at "our Camp on the Flat Head River." (Yale Collection of Western Americana, Beinecke Rare Book and Manuscript Library.)

Other illustrations:

Acknowledgments

I am grateful to the North Dakota Humanities Council, the Colorado Endowment for the Humanities, and the Minnesota Humanities Commission for giving me the opportunity to develop teacher institutes that have, among other things, explored the life and character of Meriwether Lewis.

Lewis and Clark College of Portland, Oregon, generously made available images from its special collections for use in illustrating this monograph. Lewis and Clark College is rapidly emerging as one of the primary Lewis and Clark research centers in the United States. Doug Erickson and Roger Wendlick have been unfailingly helpful.

This is a humanities essay, an expression of a perspective I have learned over the course of twenty years thanks to the existence of the National Endowment for the Humanities, the most Jeffersonian institution in America, and its state partners, the state humanities councils. There are only two things I would not wish to live without, my daughter Catherine and the humanities. The NEH and state councils have been my home institution.

I am grateful to Sally McBeth, Maggie Coval, Cheryl Dickson, James Holmberg, Craig Buthold, Holly Bard, Robert Bunting, Mike Jacobs, Jim Fuglie, Mike Waldera, Michele Basta, Janet Daley, Peter Sellers, Kent Zimmerman, Greg Jacobs, Gary Zacuto, Rebecca Luna, and Celeste Campbell.

Everyone who loves Lewis and Clark is indebted to Stephen E. Ambrose, who, with the genius Ken Burns, brought the story back into national prominence on the eve of the Expedition's bicentennial. Professor Ambrose and his family have been unendingly generous to me.

My greatest intellectual debt is to James Ronda, who wrote the only book you must not fail to read if you wish to understand Lewis and Clark: *Lewis and Clark Among the Indians* (Lincoln and London: University of Nebraska Press, 1984).

My former student Anne Rawlinson-Jacobs read the manuscript and improved it in important ways. Diane Ives found and checked facts. Janie Guill made it all happen. Long ago, Etta L. Walker, md. jr. gave me the best insight into the character of Meriwether Lewis I ever received.

In the field Becky Cawley, Cindy Lewis, Otter Woman, and Harlan and Barb Opdahl have guided me to the Pacific and back again. Becky Cawley got me lost. The incomparable Stephen Dow Beckham of Lewis and Clark College showed me what a public humanities scholar can be. His is the standard against which I measure myself. He has opened doors that have changed my life. Like heroes we have soaked in the warm springs of the Lolo Trail.

Above all, I want to thank three individuals. Patti Perry of Marmarth, North Dakota, patched me together and showed Homeric hospitality when I straggled wounded into her village during my own voyage of discovery on the Little Missouri River. Given the opportunity, she would have whupped Meriwether Lewis into mental health. My mother Mil Jenkinson has been the steadier cocaptain through most of my travel adventures. She is one of the Little Missouri River's chief admirers. Most important, Everett C. Albers taught me how to see through the lens of the humanities. This essay owes more to great-hearted Everett Albers than to any other person.

Clay Jenkinson
September 23, 2000

Background

It was the brainchild of Thomas Jefferson. The Third President had convinced Congress to appropriate funds for what became the Lewis and Clark Expedition even before the news of the Louisiana Purchase reached the United States in July of 1803. Jefferson selected a neighbor and fellow Virginian, Meriwether Lewis, to lead the Expedition. Lewis in turn selected his friend William Clark to serve as co-commander.

Lewis received a short course in Enlightenment science from President Jefferson in the White House, where he served as correspondence secretary for eighteen months between 1801-1803, and from Jefferson's scientific friends in Philadelphia. He gathered supplies in Philadelphia, Harper's Ferry and Pittsburgh. He left Pittsburgh in a specially-constructed keelboat on August 31, 1803, and floated down the entire length of the Ohio River to its junction with the Mississippi. The Expedition was thus a continental adventure. At Clarksville, Indiana Territory, Lewis caught up with William Clark on October 15, 1803. Together they collected men at army posts and wilderness clearings until their company had swelled far beyond the ten to twelve men authorized by Congress.

The Expedition spent three winters in the wilderness. The first winter camp was built at the mouth of the Missouri River on the Illinois side. It was called Camp Wood. Clark spent the winter of 1803 preparing the men for their adventure while Lewis gathered information in St. Louis. The Expedition left St. Louis on May 14, 1804 in three boats: the fifty-five foot keelboat, and two flat-bottomed pirogues. In the first season of travel Lewis and Clark ascended the Missouri from its mouth to the center of North Dakota, where they wintered among Mandan and Hidatsa Indians at the Great Bend of the Missouri River. They called their quarters Fort Mandan.

In 1805 the Expedition pressed west into what Meriwether Lewis considered *terra incognita*. The cumbersome keelboat was sent back to St. Louis. Now the flotilla consisted of six small canoes and the two pirogues. By June 13, Lewis and Clark had reached the Great Falls of the Missouri River, and by August 11 its "source" in extreme southwestern Montana. In the fall of 1805 Lewis and Clark threaded their way through the Bitterroot Mountains, which proved to be the most difficult portion of the journey in both directions. By mid-November the Expedition had descended the Clearwater-Snake-Columbia basin to the Pacific Ocean.

Lewis and Clark spent their third winter near the mouth of the Columbia at an encampment they called Fort Clatsop. It was a miserable winter. Lewis wrote scientific essays. Clark worked on his map. Late in March 1806, they began their return journey. Although they were by now bankrupt of trade goods, weary of travel, impatient with Indians, and although they were held up by the snowpack in the Bitterroot Mountains, Lewis and Clark managed to reach St. Louis by September 23, 1806.

The return journey was especially difficult for Meriwether Lewis. Exploring the upper reaches of the Marias River in late July, his reconnaissance party of four was forced to kill two Blackfeet warriors who were attempting to steal their guns and horses. On August 11, 1806, near what is now Williston, North Dakota, Lewis was accidentally shot in the buttocks by one of his men, Pierre Cruzatte.

The Expedition traveled 7689 miles. Lewis is credited with discovering 178 plant and 122 animal species. He met with more than fifty Indian tribes. Clark's 1814 map of the American West was a monumental achievement.

Thomas Jefferson appointed Lewis to the governorship of Louisiana Territory. Lewis was dilatory in taking up his post. He was, by all accounts, a poor governor. He had developed a severe drinking problem. He was on his way to Monticello and Washington, D.C., on October 11, 1809, when he apparently committed suicide. He is buried seventy-two miles from Nashville, Tennessee. At the time of his death, at thirty-five, Lewis had not written a single page of his proposed three-volume narrative of the Expedition.

A Note on the Quotations

Lewis and Clark were colorful spellers. They played fast and loose with English grammar, and they frequently ignored the niceties of punctuation and capitalization. They were writing field journals, not polished prose. We are fortunate to have their undigested journal entries, which keep alive the strained wilderness circumstances of their origin.

I have chosen to print quotations just as they appear in the definitive University of Nebraska Press edition of *The Journals of Lewis & Clark Expedition*, edited by Gary Moulton. I have attempted to make as few editorial intrusions as possible. Occasionally I place the correct word in brackets within a quotation, but only if the meaning of the passage would otherwise be obscure. And rather than note misspellings with the usual editorial notation [sic], I have been extremely rigorous in my proofreading. Readers can trust that the irregularities in the text reflect what Lewis and Clark wrote, not printing errors.

Readers should not assume that Meriwether Lewis and William Clark were ignorant men just because they were weak spellers. Standards were less rigorous in their day (even for Thomas Jefferson) and they were writing under extreme conditions. They carried a small library across the American continent, but not a dictionary.

Bad spellers are phonetically reliable. Since they have not yielded to orthographical conventions, they often spell words more or less as they pronounce them. It is delightful to consider that William Clark probably called mosquitoes "Muskeetors" and moccasins "mockersons."

Clay Jenkinson

Introduction

When he straggled into Grinder's Inn, seventy-two miles from Nashville, Tennessee, on the last melancholy journey of his life, Meriwether Lewis was offered a bed for the night. He refused it. Lewis informed Mrs. Grinder, the proprietor of the crude hostelry he had happened upon on the Natchez Trace, that since his return from the Missouri country he no longer found comfort in a featherbed. He had become accustomed, he said, to sleeping on the floor. That said, he asked his free black servant Pernier to bring in bear skins and a buffalo robe and spread them on the floor. Meriwether Lewis did not sleep on the last night of his life, October 10-11, 1809.

If a bed is one symbol of what "the hand of civilization has prepared for us" [January 1, 1806], Meriwether Lewis never fully re-entered American life after his Voyage of Discovery.

He was, of course, brave, resourceful, intelligent and persistent. He provided nearly flawless leadership of the Corps of Discovery between July 1803 and September 23, 1806. He led more than thirty men (and a woman and infant child) across the continent to the Pacific Ocean and back again, often through country that was virtually or entirely unknown to European man, hundreds and at times thousands of miles from any hope of resupply. In the course of the three-year Expedition, only one member of his company died (of disease), and only two Indians were killed in a skirmish that was precipitated by Blackfeet warriors and not by members of Lewis's command. His judgment in crisis was remarkably sound. Whatever his private forebodings, he never failed to find the courage and resolution to make the best of circumstances. When he kept a journal he was capable of writing passages of extraordinary detail, sophistication, and even lyricism. He was a brilliant amateur scientist. Thomas Jefferson recognized in Lewis "firmness of constitution & character, prudence, habits adapted to the woods, & a familiarity with the Indian manners & character, requisite for this undertaking."[1]

> *"Altho' no regular botanist &c. he possesses a remarkable store of accurate observation on all the subjects of the three kingdoms, & will therefore readily single out whatever presents itself new to him in either: and he has qualified himself for taking those observations of longitude & latitude necessary to fix the geography of the line he passes through."*
>
> — Jefferson to Benjamin Smith Barton, February 27, 1803

All that is the stuff of American myth. My purpose is not to go over that well-trodden ground. I will focus instead on some less well-known characteristics of Meriwether Lewis, the delights, the oddities, the quirks and even the dark sides of his character, not because I wish to provide a distorted picture of a man who deserves to be considered an American hero, but rather to tease out qualities of his soul that may illuminate his unusual personality and possibly even help to explain why he committed suicide in the early morning hours of 11 October 1809 at a lonely inn in Tennessee. It seems to me that the central fact of the story of Meriwether Lewis is his mental breakdown and suicide in 1809. Most students of American history never learn that he died prematurely, much less that his whole world had crumbled in the last year of his thirty-five-year life. One indication of the way Lewis has been simplified, indeed mythologized in American history is the invariable hendiadys "Lewis-and-Clark." Lewis and Clark have been welded together in phrase as well as in the American mind. The phrase "Lewis and Clark" seems to connote interchangeable heroes in fringed buckskin on a twenty-eight-month camping trip in the American West. The truth is more complicated and infinitely more interesting. Meriwether Lewis and William Clark were different sorts of men. Clark lived a full life. Clark was married (twice). Clark had children. Clark completed his tasks. Clark wrote his name on trees. Clark was America's Everyman.[2]

So who was Meriwether Lewis? Is it possible at this remove to excavate the man from the rubble of American myth?

The character of Meriwether Lewis needs to be probed from the inside out. Partly because Lewis's journals were never revised for publication, they are remarkably revealing documents. If Lewis had known that whatever he jotted into the journals would fix his character forever in the eyes of the world, he would undoubtedly have engaged in much more self-censorship than he did. If he had lived to publish his three-volume narrative of the Expedition, he would surely have touched up the persona he offered to the public. His premature and violent death in 1809 freezes him in his undigested field notes. From his own point of view, this is probably disastrous. Lewis took himself so seriously that he would almost certainly be abashed to know that he exists, in afterlife, warts and all: grammatical shortcuts, misspellings, flashes of pique and pettiness, self-doubts, fear, even the workings of his bowels on display for all the world to analyze. Lewis's pretentiousness is one of his most remarkable characteristics. Had he lived, he would probably have attenuated the earthy candor, the directness, the idiosyncratic, and the pedestrian in his journals. He would have strained for the heroic and the sublime, as he usually does in the journals when he can feel the reader over his shoulder. Sometimes it is clear that Lewis is writing the first draft of his book in the wilderness. Sometimes he is merely jotting down his field notes and impressions. We are fortunate to have both. It is the undigestedness of the journals that make them so marvelous, and so revealing of the complexities of his character.

Jefferson's favorite ancient biographer Plutarch argued that the character of great men is more often revealed in the little things than in their heroic actions. In the *Life of Alexander*, Plutarch wrote, "Nor is it always in the most distinguished achievements that men's virtues or vices may be best discerned; but very often an action of small note, a short saying, or a jest, shall distinguish a person's real character more than the greatest sieges, or the most important battles."[3] The journals of Meriwether Lewis as we have them constitute a gold mine of Plutarchian minutiae. They offer an excellent window on Lewis's strange, remarkable soul.

My plan is to set aside the perception of Meriwether Lewis as "epic explorer" and attempt to view him through a fresh lens. I intend to pore over the fragments he has left us to see what they reveal about his character. My focus is "all things great and small," but it makes sense to begin with the small. In attempting to tease

Plutarch (ca. 45-125 C.E.) was a prolific biographer and essayist. His Parallel Lives *inspired several of Shakespeare's plays, including* Julius Caesar *and* Antony and Cleopatra. *His influence on the American Republic in the age of Jefferson was enormous. The Founding Fathers shaped their own characters in the pages of Plutarch. Most Americans read Plutarch in John Dryden's 1683-86 translation. Jefferson, of course, read Plutarch in the original Greek.*

Plutarch set out to do more than chronicle historical events. His purpose was to examine minutely the character of great men and to offer his insights as a lesson for the living. Plutarch was thus a moral historian. Although he had some access to old manuscripts, he read history with caution, and his focus was always on the apparently insignificant gestures, encounters, sayings, and anecdotes that in fact opened windows on the character of great historical figures. In the Life of Pericles, *he writes, "It is so hard to find out the truth of anything by looking at the record of the past. The process of time obscures the truth of former times, and even contemporaneous writers disguise and twist the truth out of malice or flattery."*

out something as elusive as the character of a man who has been dead for almost two hundred years, I will necessarily speculate a good deal in the course of this essay, particularly when I examine the sudden death of Meriwether Lewis. I assume that readers will trust my presentation of facts, embrace what makes sense of my analysis, and cheerfully discard that which fails to convince.

Adaptations of drawings made by Charles B.J. Févret de Saint- Mémin of William Clark (right) and Meriwether Lewis (left) were printed in color for the cover of the 1904 edition of Reuben Gold Thwaites Original Journals of the Lewis and Clark Expedition 1804-1806. *The initial fifteen-volume edition was limited to fifty sets.*

Physiognomy

William Strickland copied Charles B.J. Févret de Saint-Mémin's in this 1816 acquatint of Meriwether Lewis.

There was something rather stiff about Meriwether Lewis. Peachy Gilmer, Lewis's boyhood classmate at the log school of Parson Matthew Maury in Virginia, provides a portrait of the explorer as a young man. Lewis was, he writes, "always remarkable for perseverance, which in the early period of his life seemed nothing more than obstinacy in pursuing the trifles that employ that age; a martial temper; great steadiness of purpose, self-possession, and undaunted courage. His person was stiff and without grace; bowlegged, awkward, formal, and almost without flexibility. His face was comely and by many considered handsome."[4] This is an insightful portrait of Meriwether Lewis. Most of the elements of his adult character are noted here: perseverance, obstinacy, martial temperament, steadiness of purpose, courage, self-possession, inflexibility, formality. Plus bowed legs. Although Gilmer clearly admires Lewis, his portrait is not entirely flattering. Given what we know about the last decade of Lewis's life, Gilmer's suggestion that Lewis later overcame some of his immaturities is not convincing.

Though his assessment was written in retrospect, Gilmer is reconstructing Lewis in his youth. His was a friend's and classmate's assessment. At the other end of Lewis's foreshortened life, his subordinate and enemy Frederick Bates provided a remarkably similar evaluation. From St. Louis, Bates wrote to his brother, "How unfortunate for this man that he resigned his commission in the army: His habits are altogether military & he never can I think succeed in any other profession."[5] Bates's assessment dovetails with Stephen Ambrose's argument that Thomas Jefferson erred in naming Lewis to the governorship of Louisiana, a civilian post.[6] It also reinforces the idea that Lewis had great difficulty re-entering American life after his return from the Missouri country.

Stiffness is the physiognomy of Lewis in the journals of the Expediting. It is clear that the Captain kept himself aloof. He appears most alive when he is alone on the shore with his gun, his notebook, and his Newfoundland dog Seaman. He makes it clear that he did not share in the convivialities of the Expedition. He often informs us that the men danced under the light of the moon, but if he ever joined the dance, neither he nor other journalists mentions it. Unlike virtually everyone else, Lewis routinely declines Indian sexual hospitality. When he cooks a meal, wears a knapsack, carries a load, or paddles a boat, Lewis goes out of his way to inform his readers that he is breaking character. Part of this is the decorum of military command, part of it a reflection of personality. When the Shoshone chief Cameahwait invades Lewis's private space, the Captain stiffly grumbles that he grew "heartily tired of the national hug" [August 13, 1805]. There is something unbending in the character of Meriwether Lewis. If Clark defines himself as first among equals, Lewis presents himself as a man apart.

Clothes Horse

Lewis was vain and prickly about his clothes. Although he seems to have adjusted well enough to life in animal skins — something Jefferson once admitted he could not contemplate for himself[7] — Lewis wanted his official clothing to be punctiliously correct. Before the Expedition, when he was a young army officer stationed in the (Ohio) West, he experienced what can only be described as a hissy fit over a botched uniform coat. To his friend Frederick L. Claiborne he wrote on January 15, 1798,

> Of all the damned pieces of work, my coat exceeds. It would take up three sheets of paper, written in shorthand, to point out its deficiencies or, I may even say, deformities. However, let it suffice that he has not lined the body at all; he had galoon furnished for that purpose. The lace is deficient. I had it taken to pieces and altered and could I have done without it I should have returned it, beyond a doubt. For the blind button holes on the cuff he substituted lace and no part of those on the facings was worked blind. The four small buttons on the cape are deficient. . . .[8]

With due allowance for military pride, it is difficult to square this portrait of a junior officer fussing over his uniform with the mythic notion of Meriwether Lewis as a cheerful buckskinner, a mountain man on the upper Missouri. It is not surprising that he was, in his young manhood, known as "the sublime dandy."[9] He was a wilderness man with a comely face.

Among the Shoshone in 1805, impatiently waiting for Clark and the main party to catch up, Lewis found ample time to study the ways and means of his hosts. Ethnology on the Expedition was largely a by-product of delay. Lewis showed a particular interest in gender relations and dress. After describing in lavish detail the typical clothing of the tribe, he took time to describe a fur robe: "The tippet of the Snake Indians is the most eligant peice of Indian dress I ever saw, the neck or collar of this is formed of a strip of dressed Otter skin with the fur. it is about four or five inches wide and is cut out of the back of the skin the nose and eyes forming one extremity and the tail the other" [August 20, 1805]. Lewis not only made sure that he obtained for himself a Shoshone tippet of precisely this description, but in 1807 he insisted upon being painted by Charles B.J.Févret de Saint-Mémin with it draped over his shoulders. Later, he donated (or loaned) the tippet to America's first museum director Charles Wilson Peale, who draped it over the wax effigy he sculpted of Lewis. For Saint-Mémin, Meriwether Lewis strikes a remarkably effeminate pose. There is something slightly ridiculous in the presentation, and yet one senses that this is precisely how Lewis wished to appear. A painting, after all, is no accidental snapshot. Lewis is a man who struck poses.

Just before the return from Fort Clatsop, the Corps of Discovery found that the Clatsops Indians would not sell a much-needed canoe for anything less than Lewis's military dress coat. The captain does not veto the bargain struck on the Expedition's behalf by Sergeant Nathaniel Pryor, but he is unmistakably petulant when he describes the transaction:

> it seems that nothing excep this coat would induce them to dispose of a canoe which in their mode of traffic is an article of the greatest val[u]e except a wife, with whom it is equal, and is generally given in exchange to the father for his daughter. I think the U' States are indebted to me another Uniform coat, for that of which I have disposed on this occasion was but little woarn [March 17, 1806].

Perhaps it is less remarkable that Lewis had to give up his beloved officer's coat to get his company back to civilization than that he still *had* a dress uniform this far along in the Expedition's travels. Perhaps it was partly his resentment over the loss of his prize officer's coat that induced Captain Lewis to justify — in the same journal entry — stealing a Clatsop canoe, "in lue of the six Elk which they stole from us in the winter." When Lewis finally submitted his accounts to the War Department in the summer of 1807, he requested reimbursement for "One Uniform Laced Coat, one silver Epaulet, one Dirk, & belt, one hanger & belt, one pistol & one fowling piece, all private property, given in exchange for Canoe, Horses &c. for public service during the Expedition — $135."[10]

If clothes make the man, we can imagine how disturbing it must have been for Meriwether Lewis to be stripped — piece by piece — of all the trappings of civilization and authority. The prize coat had symbolic value far exceeding its cost. It was, for him, a

Lewis and Clark hired a carpenter, a blacksmith, a fisherman, a tailor, and hunters and interpreters, to cross the continent, but not an artist. Both Lewis and Clark penned sketches of flora and fauna and artifacts into their journals, but they made no attempt to draw the West in a more systematic way.

At the Great Falls in Montana, Lewis lamented his lack of both verbal and artistic talents.

The drawing at the right is from the fourth edition of Sergeant Patrick Gass's Journal of the Voyages and Travels of a Corps of Discovery, *published in Philadelphia in 1812. The woodcut of Lewis in uniform giving his famous speech to the Indians is one of six woodcuts in the editions published by Matthew Carey in 1810, 1811, and 1812. First published in Pittsburgh in 1807, Gass was also published in London (1808), France (1810), and Germany (1812). The woodcuts became standard illustrations in later editions of journals of the Corps of Discovery.*

marker of rank, of authority, of achievement, of civilization, even of identity. The War Department could pay, but it is not clear that it could compensate. If it is mythically appropriate that the hero should return to his home like Odysseus, essentially naked and destitute, after a soul-transforming journey into a far country, it was probably not — for Lewis — very satisfying to do so. The Expedition arrived back in St. Louis on September 23, 1806. One day later Lewis and Clark visited a tailor.[11]

Charles B.J. Févret de Saint-Mémin's sketches of Meriwether Lewis — most likely, one completed in 1802 and the other either just before or soon after his journey to the Pacific — were done with the help of a contraption invented in France by Gilles-Louis Chrétien, the physiognotrace ("physionotrace" in French). Saint-Mémin sold customers a package of images which included the original drawing, plate, and twelve engravings. Lewis engaged Saint-Mémin to do "likenesses of Indians" for his intended publication of the journals.

The one at the right could have been completed after Lewis's return, although it does bear remarkable resemblance to a silhoutte at Monticello dated 1803 and a reversed image in the National Portrait Gallery of the Smithsonian Institution bearing the date 1803. The engraving at the left came from a lost drawing probably done in 1802, photographed at the turn of the century in Richmond, Virginia, by H.P. Cook. For the most authoritative discussion of Saint-Mémin's images of Lewis, see Ellen G. Miles, Saint-Mémin and the Neoclassical Profile Portrait in America, *pp. 338-340.*

Dining Out: Eating the West

Meriwether Lewis loved to eat. And, apparently, to talk about it. After some lean days among the emaciated Shoshone, Lewis confesses that he "arrose very early and as hungary as a wolf!" [August 15, 1805]. It is true that he had not had a square meal for several days when he made this remark, but one senses that hunger was not the only issue. Food was a central concern for the commander of the Voyage of Discovery. No other journalist writes so often, so lavishly, and so lovingly about food. Lewis is not content to obtain provender. One of the ways he explores the West is to ingest it. His palate is one of his primary lenses on the wilderness. Like an infant, he discovered his world by way of his mouth. At an alkaline creek in eastern Montana on May 23, 1805, Lewis writes, "I have tryed it by way of experiment & find it moderately pergative, but painfull to the intestens in it's opperation." This is a characteristic gesture. When in doubt, ingest.

Lewis seems to have considered himself something of a food epicure. Perhaps this was an inevitability after spending two years living in Thomas Jefferson's White House.[12] Jefferson spent $2797.28 on wine alone in the first year of his presidency, and $6508.55 on groceries and provisions — out of a salary of $25,000.[13]

So lavish was he with French wines and foods after the Paris sojourn (1784-89) that Patrick Henry grumbled that Jefferson had "abjured his native victuals."[14] Like almost everyone else, Lewis seems to have come under the spell of Jefferson's republican hospitality code: French wines, French cuisine, exquisite desserts and conversations, and unpretentious elegance. Dignified pell-mell. Whatever the cause, Lewis spends much more time than Clark reflecting on the Expedition's diet, and indeed on the social, physiological, and even philosophical implications of the food the Corps ingested in the American West.

Thus after writing a long technical description of the *pomme blanche* (*Psoralea esculenta*) of eastern Montana, admired by Indians and the French engagés alike, Lewis concludes: "the white apple appears to me to be a tastless insippid food of itself, tho' I have no doubt but it is a very healthy and moderately nutricious food. I have no doubt but our epicures would admire this root very much, it would serve them in their ragouts and gravies in stead of the truffles morella" [May 8, 1805]. Lewis may well have his mentor Thomas Jefferson in mind here. There may be humor, even some sarcasm, in his claim that "our epicures would admire this root" in spite of the

After offending the British Ambassador Anthony Merry and his wife with his democratic White House protocol in 1803, and nearly provoking an international incident, Thomas Jefferson wrote a Presidential directive on hospitality. "When brought together in society, all are perfectly equal, whether foreign or domestic, titled or untitled, in or out of office. At public ceremonies, to which the government invites the presence of foreign ministers and their families, a convenient seat or station will be provided for them, with any other strangers invited and the families of the national ministers, each taking place as they arrive, and without any precedence. To maintain the principle of equality, or of pele mela, and prevent the growth of precedence out of courtesy, the members of the Executive will practice at their own houses, and recommend an adherence to the ancient usage of the country, of gentlemen in mass giving precedence to the ladies in mass, in passing from one apartment where they are assembled into another."

— Thomas Jefferson,
A Memorandum
(Rules of Etiquette), 1803.

fact that he finds it a "tasteless insippid food." Perhaps Lewis is merely missing the President's lavish table. Perhaps he is indulging the rugged man's sense of superiority over the palates of over-civilized men. *De gustibus non est disputandum.*[15]

Like — or perhaps because of — his patron Thomas Jefferson, Lewis had a propensity for statistics. In the Great Falls country of Montana, he writes: "we eat an emensity of meat; it requires 4 deer, an Elk and a deer, or one buffaloe, to supply us pentifully 24 hours. meat now forms our food prinsipally as we reserve our flour parched meal and corn as much as possible for the rocky mountains which we are shortly to enter, and where from the indian accounts, game is not very abundant" [July 13, 1805]. On April 27, 1805, at the confluence of the Missouri and Yellowstone Rivers, Lewis writes: "altho' the game is very abundant and gentle, we only kill as much as is necessary for food. I believe that two good hunters could conveniently supply a regiment with provisions." On May 5, 1805 he adds: " . . . we kill whatever we wish." On May 6: "it is now only amusement for Capt. C. and myself to kill as much meat as the party can consum; I hope it may continue thus through our whole rout, but this I do not much expect." Lewis and Clark were awestruck by the cornucopia of Montana. It was Eden then.

The living was not so easy on the other side of the Rocky Mountains. During the lean winter at Fort Clatsop, Lewis reports: " . . . no one seems much concerned about the state of the stores; so much for habit. we have latterly so frequently had our stock of provisions reduced to a minimum and sometimes taken a small touch of fasting that three days full allowance excites no concern" [January 20, 1806]. By now everyone knew that if game existed and Drewyer[16] was healthy, the Expedition would be well fed.

Lewis approved of boiled antelope and roasted salmon (" . . . both of which I eat with a very good relish") [August 13, 1805], buffalo calf ("I think it equal to any veal I ever tasted") [April 21, 1805], squirrel ("I made my dog take as many each day as I had occasion for, they wer fat and I thought them when fryed a pleasent food—") [September 11, 1803], and he positively gushed over beaver tail: " . . . the flesh of the beaver is esteemed a delecacy among us;. I think the tale a most delicious morsal, when boiled, it resembles in flavor the fresh tongues and sounds of the codfish, and is usually sufficiently large to afford a plentifull meal for two men" [May 2, 1805]. Lewis reports, " . . . the men prefer the flesh of this anamal to that of any other which we have, or are able to procure, at the moment. I eat heartily of the beaver myself, and think it excellent, particularly the tale, and liver" [April 17, 1805]. On May 16, 1805, he reports: "we caught two Antelopes at our encampment in attempting to swim the river; these animals are but lean as yet, and of course not very pleasant food. I walked on shore this evening and killed a buffaloe cow and calf, we found the calf most excellent veal."

At Fort Clatsop Lewis was able to report, "our fare is the flesh of lean elk boiled with pure water and a little salt. the whale blubber, which we have used very sparingly, is now exhausted. on this food I do not feel strong, but enjoy the most perfect health;— [Notice the nice distinction — Lewis has *theories* of nutrition.] a keen appetite supplys in a great degree the want of more luxurious sauses or dishes, and still render my ordinary meals not uninteresting to me, for I find myself sometimes enquiring of the cook whether dinner or breakfast is ready—" [January 29, 1806]. Among other things this is a delightful glimpse into daily life at Fort Clatsop. There is a gust for life in Meriwether Lewis in spite of his posture of formality and in spite of his constitutional melancholy. Had he lived to revise his journals, I doubt that Lewis would have permitted us to see the American Columbus inquiring when dinner will be ready.

Lewis was fascinated by whale. The blubber, he writes, was "white & not unlike the fat of Poark, tho' the texture was more spongey and somewhat coarser. I had a part of it cooked and found it very pallitable and tender, it resembled the beaver or the dog in flavour" [January 5, 1806]. Blubber, the other white meat!

The eulachon (candlefish) run of 1806 evokes in Lewis a tiny dissertation on his taste in fish. "I find them best when cooked in

Indian stile, which is by roasting a number of them together on a wooden spit without any previous preparation whatever. they are so fat they require no additional sauce, and I think them superior to any fish I ever tasted, even more delicate and lussious than the white fish of the lakes which have heretofore formed my standart of excellence among the fishes." Now Lewis becomes positively effete. "I have heard the fresh anchovey much extolled but I hope I shall be pardoned for believing this quite as good" [February 24, 1806]. Is this a field journal or a food column?

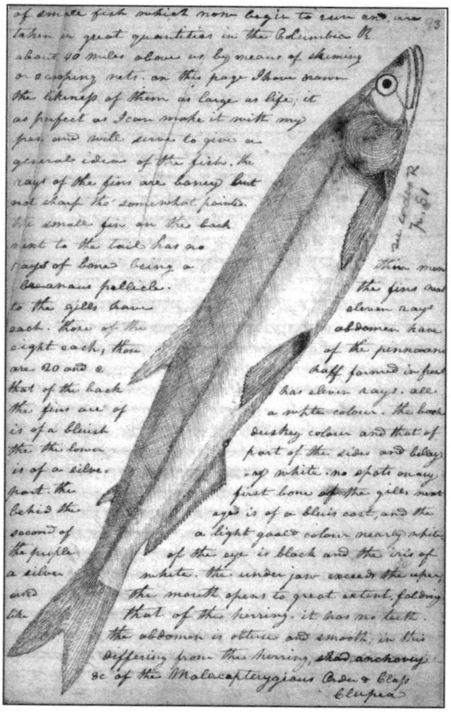

". . . on this page,' writes Lewis on February 24, 1806, "I have drawn the likeness of them [eulachon] as large as life; it as perfect as I can make it with my pen and will serve to give a general idea of the fish. . . ."

Readers of the Journals of Lewis and Clark lament that Lewis did not attempt more drawings. He has more talent than he thinks.

He also went out of his way to praise the Oregon sheldrake: "to the epicure of those parts of the union where this duck abounds nothing need be added in praise of the exquisite flavor of this duck. I have frequently eaten of them in several parts of the Union and I think those of the Columbia equally as delicious" [March 9, 1806]. The "epicure of the Union," presumably, is not the stoic vegetarian Thomas Jefferson, but his protégé Meriwether Lewis.

Lewis is the only member of the Expedition who admits to dinner preferences. On May 14, 1805 he writes, "I felt an inclination to eat some veal and walked on shore and killed a very fine buffaloe calf and a large woolf. . . ." The West was his larder. Lewis shopped with his gun.

A slight difference of opinion (at Fort Clatsop) about the desirability of salt sends Lewis into a philosophical revery. A new supply of salt, Lewis writes,

> . . . was a great treat to myself and most of the party, having not had any since the 20th ultmo.; I say most of the party, for my friend Capt. Clark declares it to be a mear matter of indifference with him whether he uses it or not; for myself I must confess I felt a considerable inconvenience from the want of it; the want of bread I consider as trivial provided, I get fat meat, for as to the species of meat I am not very particular, the flesh of the dog the horse the wolf, having from habit become equally formiliar with any other, and I have learned to think that if the chord be sufficiently strong, which binds the soul and boddy together, it dose not so much matter about the materials which compose it [January 5, 1806].

Lewis was so fond of salt that on the lean return journey of 1806 he kept back a small canister of the salt produced at Fort Clatsop so that he would have a supply for his reconnaissance trip to the northern branches of the Marias River. Epicure or no, Lewis, like the philosopher Diogenes the Cynic, claims that he eats merely to banish hunger. "The chord . . . which binds the soul and boddy to-

John Donne (1572- 1631) was a contemporary of Shakespeare. Witty, erotic, cynical, deliberately unmelliflous, Donne was the greatest of the Metaphysical Poets. He was also the greatest Anglican preacher of his age. In his Meditations Upon Emergent Occasions, *Donne gave us the phrase, "no man is an island, entire of itself . . . any man's death diminishes me. . . . and therefore never send to know for whom the bell tolls; it tolls for thee"* (Meditation xvii)*.*

Samuel Johnson (1709-1784) was the British literary dictator of his age. Johnson and Thomas Jefferson had several friends in common, but they never met and they would have disliked each other intensely. In his famous Lives of the Poets *(1781), Johnson attacked the Metaphysical Poets, including Donne: "The metaphysical poets were men of learning, and to shew their learning was their whole endeavour; but, unluckily resolving to shew it in rhyme, instead of writing poetry, they only wrote verses, and very often such verses as stood the trial of the finger better than of the ear; for the modulation was so imperfect, that they were only found to be verses by counting the syllables."*

gether," is reminiscent of lines from "The Funeral" by the Elizabethan poet John Donne:

> For if the sinewy thread my brain lets fall
> Through every part
> Can ties those parts, and make me one of all. . .

I am not suggesting, of course, that Meriwether Lewis had read John Donne. Thanks to the grumpy Dr. Johnson, nobody did (see page 17).

Because Lewis and Clark are notorious for harmony, it is remarkable that two of their rare disagreements involve food. Lewis likes salt. Clark is indifferent. Clark detests dog flesh. Lewis finds it rather delicious. On the first occasion when he is offered dog — among the Teton Sioux in late September 1804 — Clark writes tersely, " . . . raw Dog Sioux think great dish—used on festivals. eat little of dog. . ." [September 26, 1804]. On the Columbia, where dog played an essential role in the Expedition's diet, William Clark moaned, " . . . all the Party have greatly the advantage of me, in as much as they all relish the flesh of the dogs" [October 10, 1805]. In his journal Clark confesses, " . . . as for my own part, I have not become reconsiled to the taste of this animal as yet" [January 3, 1806]. Dog, horse, wolf, whale — for Meriwether Lewis it is all one.

And yet — in spite of this indifference as to the source of his protein — Lewis seldom looks on food as mere provender. Others eat. Meriwether Lewis dines. On February 7, 1806, at Fort Clatsop, he writes, "This evening we had what I call an excellent supper it consisted of a marrowbone a piece and a brisket of boiled Elk that had the appearance of a little fat on it. this for Fort Clatsop is living in high stile." Unlike most of the men with whom he traveled, Meriwether Lewis knew what "high stile" could be. And he clearly missed it.

Summarizing the winter at Fort Clatsop, Lewis waxes philosophical: "Altho' we have not fared sumptuously this winter and spring at Fort Clatsop, we have lived quite as comfortably as we had any reason to expect we should" [March 20, 1806].

On the first Marias reconnaissance, Lewis writes: "we roasted and eat a hearty supper of our venison not having taisted a mosel before during the day; I now laid myself down on some willow boughs to a comfortable nights rest, and felt indeed as if I was fully repaid for the toil and pain of the day, so much will a good shelter, a dry bed, and comfortable supper revive the sperits of the waryed, wet and hungry traveler—" [June 7, 1805]. One source of Lewis's greatness is his ability to articulate the universal experience of the wilderness. Nobody who has ever been camping fails to resonate with Lewis's conclusion.

William Clark does not write much about food. We know he was indifferent to salt, and could not stomach dog. Beyond that, we learn that he found steelhead trout[17] " . . . one of the most delicious fish I have ever tasted" [October 26, 1805]. And not much more.

Lewis seems to have spent a good deal of time thinking about what people were eating back in civilization. On July 4, 1805, at the Great Falls of the Missouri, for example, Lewis writes: " . . . we had no just cause to covet the sumptuous feasts of our countrymen on this day.—" The menu? Beans, bacon, buffalo steaks, and suet dumplings. Also, the last of the whiskey. It was the nation's twenty-ninth birthday.

Camping alone on the day he "discovers" the Great Falls, Lewis writes: "my fare is really sumptuous this evening; buffaloe's humps, tongues and marrowbones, fine trout parched meal pepper and salt, and a good appetite; the last is not considered the least of the luxuries" [June 13, 1805]. He's right. It does sound "really sumptuous." The thought of Meriwether Lewis camping virtually alone in the heart of the unspoiled American West, and like a refined bachelor cooking an elaborate dinner for himself, and then describing it with literary relish, is one of the most endearing — and romantic — images of the Expedition.

With the entire company stretched thin and working harder than ever at the Great Falls, amid scorching heat, prickly pears, grizzly bears, freak hail storms, Lewis took a turn as company cook. He announces with pride that "to myself I assign the duty of cook as well for those present as for the party which I expect again to arrive this evening from the lower camp. I collected my wood and water, boiled a large quantity of excellent dryed buffalo meat, and made each man a large suet dumpling by way of a treat" [June 26, 1805]. This is one of the most delightful entries in the journals of Lewis and Clark. It is remarkable that the commander of the Voyage of Discovery would descend to cookery. It is impossible to entertain a negative view of an army officer who makes dumplings for his men by way of a treat.

The greatest of all of Lewis's food passages is his description of the otherwise worthless Charbonneau's one real contribution to the Expedition, his buffalo hagus. On Thursday May 9, 1805 Lewis takes the time to provide a full — and hilarious — description of Charbonneau's *pièce de résistance*.

> . . . and from the cow I killed we saved the necessary materials for making what our wrighthand cook Charbono calls the *boudin blanc,* and immediately set him about preparing them for supper; this white pudding we all esteem one of the greatest delacies of the forrest, it may not be amiss therefore to give it a place. About 6 feet of the lower extremity of the large gut of the Buffaloe is the first mosel that the cook makes love to, this he holds fast at one end with the right hand, while with the forefinger and thumb of the left he gently compresses it, and discharges what he says *is not good to eat*, but of which in the squel we get a moderate portion; the mustle lying underneath the shoulder blade next to the back, and fillets are next saught, these are needed up very fine with a good portion of kidney suit; to this composition is then added a just proportion of pepper and salt and a small quantity of flour; thus far advanced, our skilfull opporator C--o seizes his recepticle, which has never once touched the water, for that would intirely distroy the regular order of the whole procedure; you will not forget that the side you now see is that covered with a good coat of fat provided the anamal be in good order; the operator sceizes the recepticle I say, and tying it fast at one end turns it inwards and begins now with repeated evolutions of the hand and arm, and a brisk motion of the finger and thumb to put in what he says is *bon pour manger*; thus by stuffing and compressing he soon distends the recepticle to the utmost limmits of it's power of expansion, and in the course of <the opperation the> it's longtudinal progress it

> drives from the other end of the recepticle a much larger portion of the ____ than was prevously discharged by the finger and thumb of the left hand in a former part of the operation; thus when the sides of the recepticle are skilfully exchanged the outer for the inner, and all is compleately filled with something good to eat, it is tyed at the other end, but not any cut off, for that would make the pattern too scant; it is then baptised in the missouri with two dips and a flirt, and bobbed into the kettle; from whence, after it be well boiled it is taken and fryed with bears oil untill it becomes brown, when it is ready to esswage the pangs of a keen appetite or such as travelers in the wilderness are seldom at a loss for.—

This is exquisite, proof that Meriwether Lewis had at times a great sense of humor. The delightfulness of this passage comes from two things. First, there is Lewis's comic portrait of the Frenchman Charbonneau making love to a buffalo gut, baptizing it in the muddy Missouri river, differentiating between what is *not good to eat* and what is *bon pour manger.* The French phrase is a great touch. It is almost certainly a direct quotation. Lewis's "two dips and a flirt" masterfully captures Charbonneau's comic professionalism. One senses here that Charbonneau knew he was funny.

The second source of comedy is the inherent disparity between the disgusting substance of Charbonneau's recipe and what Lewis acknowledges as its undeniably delicious taste. Lewis makes sure the reader understands that there is a fair quantity of the excremental in the final product. That Charbonneau should fuss over it with Gallic *amour propre,* when it is in fact nothing more than a section of the large intestine replete with semi-digested food, is inherently hilarious. Lewis does not here reflect on the comic omnivorousness of man (a theme of Homer's *Odyssey*), but surely part of the humor is the realization that there is something fundamentally grotesque in the digestive process, irrespective of what cut of the animal one ingests. A pudding is, after all, a sausage, and there is a kind of hint of the maxim, "If you like laws and sausages, you should never watch either one being made."[18]

It is also true that there is a fair amount of Anglo-Saxon condescension in this passage, as in so much of Lewis's humor. This is not the only time Lewis makes fun of Charbonneau's Catholicism. Lewis characteristically measures himself against the inferior religion, manners, habits, and appetites of others, particularly non-whites and non-Anglo-Americans. It would indeed be possible to read this passage as a blasphemous parody of the Mass with Charbonneau as the high priest of *boudin blanc*. Still, it is clear that Mr. Lewis is in a good mood on May 9, 1805, and there is even a kind of grudging affection for poor maligned Charbonneau. Albert Furtwangler rightly calls Charbonneau a "superb culinary artist."[19]

Boundin blanc must have been delicious. At the moment when the Corps of Discovery begins to climb into the Bitterroot Mountains, Lewis finds time to slip into bemused lamentation in his journal: "there is no fresh sighn of them [buffalo] and I begin to think that our harvest of white puddings is at an end, at least untill our return to buffaloe country" [July 24, 1805]. Earlier in the month, Lewis writes, " . . . when we leave the buffalo . . . we shal sometimes be under the necessity of fasting occasionally. and at all events the white puddings will be irretrievably lost and Sharbono out of imployment" [July 3, 1805]. Apparently, in Lewis's mind, Charbonneau has only one positive role.

This was not the end of Meriwether Lewis's culinary assault on the bison's organs of elimination. If Charbonneau's contribution was a semi-excremental buffalo pudding, George Drewyer's specialty was roasted but otherwise wholly unprocessed small intestines. At the Great Falls, Lewis reports: " . . . for the first time I ate of the small guts . . . in the Indian stile without any preperation of washing or other clensing and found them very good—" [July 16, 1805]. *Bon pour manger*!

On the Wing with the "Feathered Tribes"

Meriwether Lewis loved birds. His general capacity for natural history is acknowledged by everyone, but it is birds — not quadrupeds or plants or native peoples — that seem to have delighted him most.

Each of the captains got a bird — in 1811 Alexander Wilson named Clark's Nutcracker and Lewis's Woodpecker for the heroes (see page 26) — as if they were fully equal in ornithology. They were not. On the Voyage of Discovery, it was Meriwether Lewis who was the bird watcher.

On April 13, 1805, soon after leaving the Mandan villages, the Expedition came upon a Canada goose sitting in its nest on top of a cottonwood tree. Clark shot it, but it was Lewis who climbed that tree to inspect the nest. The thought of Captain Meriwether Lewis shinnying up a cottonwood in the presence of Clark and no doubt others, is purely delightful. When at last he climbed back to earth, he had brought with him an egg — which he then described in the journals.

When the time came to send the keelboat down river in April of 1805, Lewis let birds dominate his small selection of live specimens. In specially made cages, Lewis sent the curious President a prairie dog, a grouse, and four magpies. These creatures undertook an odyssey of staggering proportions to reach their audience with the President: with Corporal Warfington in the keelboat to St. Louis (forty-five days — 1600 miles), then in a series of other conveyances to New Orleans (three weeks, 1000 miles), where they were transferred to a ship for the journey around the tip of Florida, up the Atlantic coastal passageway, to Baltimore. From Baltimore they made their way overland to Washington, D.C. On August 12, 1805, four months after the menagerie departed from Fort Mandan, Jefferson's major domo, from the White House, wrote to the President, who was vacationing at Monticello: "I have just received by Baltimore a barrel and 4 boxes, and a kind of cage in which there is a little animal very much resembling the squirrel, and in the other a bird resembling the magpie of Europe." Thomas Jefferson first saw these creatures on October 4, 1805.

Death dominated *this* epic. Only the tenacious prairie dog and one of the four magpies had survived their immense journey. The President — a great collector of curiosities — displayed these living wonders in the White House for a few weeks, made them (literally) the centerpiece of his famous informal dinner parties. By October 22, 1805 he had sent them on to the intellectual capital of the western hemisphere, Philadelphia, where his friend Charles Wilson Peale displayed them in his Philadelphia Museum. The prairie dog was still alive as late as April 5, 1806. When the creatures died Peale stuffed them and put them on a shelf.

On the lower Marias River in June 1805, at a time when he was preoccupied with a geographical riddle that he believed might endanger the whole mission, Lewis found time to write: "when the sun began to shine today these birds appeared to be very gay and sung most inchantingly; I observed among them the brown thrush, Robbin, turtle dove, linnit goaldfinch, the large and small blackbird, wren and several other birds of less note" [June 8, 1805].

At this juncture, at the geopolitically critical confluence of the Marias and the Missouri rivers, Lewis discovered the loggerhead shrike, the sage grouse, and McCowan's longspur. Of the longspur he wrote, " . . . this bird . . . rises into the air about 60 feet and supporting itself in the air with a brisk motion of the wings sings very sweetly, has several shrill soft notes reather of the plaintive order which it frequently repeats and varies, after remaining stationary about a minute in his aireal station he descends obliquely occasionally pausing and accomnying his descension with a note something like *twit twit twit*; on the ground he is silent. thirty or forty of these birds will be stationed in the air at a time in view, these larks as I shall call them add much to the gayety and cheerfullness of the scene" [June 4, 1805]. Meriwether Lewis not only observed birds with a very discerning eye, but with obvious delight. No other journalist ever writes that birds bring "gayety and cheerfullness" to the experience.

In South Dakota Lewis writes a lavish description of the black-billed magpie, which includes measurements, an attempt to transcribe the call of the bird (eight "twaits" separated in the middle), a nearly poetic account of the way the bird's tail feathers change color depending on one's angle of observation, and an analysis of its social habits. "the tints of these feathers," Lewis writes, "are very similar and equally as beautiful and rich as the tints of blue and green of the peacock— it is a most beautifull bird—" [September 17, 1804].

There are three orders of genius here. It is one thing to provide descriptive terms so complete and precise that later ornithologists have had little trouble identifying the birds of the Expedition. It is more remarkable that the busy captain — the commander of a military party that was always moving as fast as possible through a potentially dangerous landscape — found time to expatiate on the beauty and sublimity of the birds he encountered. But most remarkable of all is Lewis's willingness to listen to and record the language of birds in the West. One pictures him standing with head cocked trying first to make out the sound of the magpie and then to render it into English orthography. This is the work of a man alone in the woods, a very extraordinary man. However odd it may seem, indeed however damaging to Meriwether Lewis's character, it appears undeniable that he was more interested in birds than in American Indians. Indians frequently annoy Captain Lewis. Birds never fail to delight him.

From May 14, 1804 to October 16, 1804 Captain Lewis maintains an unaccountable near-total silence in the journals of the Corps of Discovery, but he wakes up at the bottom of what is now North Dakota to write a field note about a bird they found that was in a state of semi-hibernation. "it appeared," he wrote, "to be passing into the dormant state. . . . I run my penknife into it's body under the wing and completely distroyed it's lungs and heart— yet it lived upwards of two hours this fanominon I could not account for

Meriwether Lewis brought back with him specimens of many of the "feathered tribe." He carried them to Philadelphia in April 1807 and asked Alexander Wilson of the American Philosophical Society for portraits to illustrate his narrative. After Lewis's death, Wilson wrote, "It was the request and particular wish of Captain Lewis made to me in person that I should make drawings of each of the feathered tribe as had been preserved, and were new."[20] Wilson made drawings of three of Lewis's birds, which he also named: the Louisiana tanager (now called "western tanager"), Clark's crow (now Clark's nutcracker), and Lewis's woodpecker. They appeared in a single plate in Volume III of Wilson's American Ornithology *(shown above — bottom: Clark's nutcracker; top-left: Western tanager; top-right: Lewis's woodpecker).*

unless it proceeded from the want of circulation of the blod" [October 16, 1804]. Thus Lewis anticipates scientific confirmation of the torpidity of the whippoorwill by almost 150 years.[21] As usual, Lewis takes down the bird's vocabulary: "at-tah-to'-nah'; at-tah'-to'-nah'; to-nah. . . ." Then, promptly, he goes back to sleep in the journals until April 1807, a fanominon no one has been able to account for.

Lewis and Clark record 134 bird species, at least thirty-four of which were new to American science.[22]

Lewis's ornithologist friend Alexander Wilson independently observed the torpidity of the whippoorwill. In the text accompanying his drawing of the "whip-poor-will," Wilson says, "In traversing the woods one day, in the early part of June, along the brow of a rocky declivity, a whip-poor-will rose from my feet, and fluttered along, sometimes prostrating herself, and beating the ground with her wings, as if just expiring. Aware of her purpose, I stood still, and began to examine the space immediately around me for the eggs or young, one or other of which I was certain must be near. After a long search, to my mortification, I could find neither; and was just going to abandon the spot, which I perceived somewhat like a slight mouldiness among the withered leaves, and, on stooping down, discovered it to be a young whip-poor will, seemingly asleep, as its eyelids were nearly closed; or perhaps this might only be to protect its tender eyes from the glare of day. I sat down by it on the leaves, and drew it as it then appeared. It was probably not a week old. All the while I was thus engaged, it neither moved its body, nor opened its eyes more than half; and I left it as I found it. After I had walked about a quarter of a mile from the spot, recollecting that I had left a pencil behind, I returned and found my pencil, but the young bird was gone."

— Alexander Wilson, *American Ornithology*, Volume V, 1812.

A Little Knowledge is a Dangerous Thing

Although Thomas Jefferson declared that Lewis was "not regularly educated,"[23] Lewis tended to display what erudition he had in the journals. There is no doubt that Lewis was an advocate of education. He had, after all, made the long journey from Georgia to Albemarle County, Virginia, at the age of thirteen primarily to obtain a formal education. He had none of the contempt for formal education of the rough and ready man. Some of this may be the work of Jefferson, the best-educated American of his time, and the greatest advocate of education in American history. Lewis spends a great deal of time in his family correspondence insisting upon a proper training for his younger brothers Reuben Lewis and John Marks. Even at the farthest outpost of the Europeanized world, from Fort Mandan, on March 31, 1805, Lewis takes time to attend to the education of his siblings. "I must request of you," he writes his mother, "before I conclude this letter, to send John Markes to the College at Williamsburgh, as soon as it shall be thought that his education has been sufficiently advanced to fit him for that ceminary; for you may rest assured that as you regard his future prosperity you had better make any sacrifice of his property than suffer his education to be neglected or remain incomple."[24] This was written in a log hut perhaps as far from a school as it was possible to be in 1805. No doubt it would please Thomas Jefferson to know that virtually the first letter ever written in North Dakota was about the importance of education!

In the famous melancholic birthday meditation of August 18, 1805, Lewis regrets his want of education as much as his lack of genuine achievement. "I reflected," he writes, "that I had as yet done but little, very little indeed, to further the hapiness of the human race or to advance the information of the succeeding generation. I viewed with regret the many hours I have spent in indolence, and now soarly feel the want of that information which those hours would have given me had they been judiciously expended." Lewis wishes he had studied more. His mentor Jefferson read between ten and fifteen hours per day when he was a young man. When the moment came, in 1776, *he* was ready to distill the entire Enlightenment into the thirty-six most important words of the English language. The imperfect protégé, at the source of the Missouri, on his thirty-first birthday, is painfully aware that when the moment comes, there is no further time for preparation. You either know how to spell "soarly" or you don't.

Clark is almost invariably straightforward in his journal entries. He writes what he has to say in the simplest language he can muster. Lewis strains after allusions, ideas, a lofty vocabulary, literary flair, and — often enough — profundity. Thus, in Montana he writes, "our trio of pests still invade and obstruct us on all occasions, these are the Musquetoes eye knats and prickley pears, equal to any three curses that ever poor Egypt laiboured under, except the *Mahometant yoke*. the men complain of being much fortiegued" [July 24, 1805]. Here Lewis mingles a bit of Biblical lore with a jingoistic assault on Islam.

On the same occasion Lewis reveals in a few words a great deal about both the distribution of labors in the Voyage of Discovery and also his concept of leadership: "the men complain of being much fortiegued, their labour is excessively great. I occasionaly encourage them by assisting in the labour of navigating the canoes, and have learned *to push a tolerable good pole* in their fraize" [July 24, 1805]. Here Lewis even manages to record what must have been the laboring men's sense of superiority over their commander, whose forays into "navigation" were surely few and far between and probably, at least in the beginning, inept. It was a democratic country, but Meriwether Lewis was a Virginia planter and the Voyage of Discovery was a military mission. It is also remarkable that Lewis would record the actual voice of the enlisted men. One can hear the boatmen telling Lewis he manages "a tolerable good pole." When the switch was on, his drive to record his experiences was unrelenting. I find myself in agreement with Stephen Ambrose on the riddle of Lewis's missing journal entries. "Writing as a biographer rather than an archivist or a historian," Ambrose says, "that is, on the basis of the internal evidence of the September [1804] entries — I am convinced that there once existed — and still may — an important body of Lewis journal entries."[26]

Meriwether Lewis's journal gaps of 702 days of 1120 include September 19 to November 10, 1803 (53 days); November 29, 1803 to May 13, 1804 (167 days); May 16, 1804 to April 7, 1805 with the exception of entries made on May 20 and September 16 and 17, 1804 (323 days); most of the period between August 27, 1805 and December 31, 1805, with entries on ten occasions (117 days); and August 13 to September 23, 1806 (42 days).[25] *Stephen Ambrose and Donald Jackson both argue that Lewis must have written more than we have, particularly in the first year of the Expedition.*

When a war party of the Shoshone comes galloping up on August 13, 1805, Lewis's imagination drifts to the vocabulary of medieval romance. "I afterwards understood that the Indians we had first seen this morning had returned and allarmed the camp; these men had come out armed cap a pe."[27] William Clark would not have used such a term.

Among the skittish Shoshone Lewis writes of, "the capricious disposition of those people who never act but from the impulse of the moment. they were now very cheerfull and gay, and two hours ago they looked as sirly as so many imps of satturn" [August 15, 1805]. Although the source of this allusion is unknown, Lewis is clearly referring to medieval humours theory. The Shoshone are saturnine — moody, pessimistic, sullen. Imps.

Lewis has a large, at times a pretentious, vocabulary. He calls earthly existence the "sublunary world" [August 18, 1805]. He observes "a large assemblage" of prairie dogs [May 23, 1805]. He reaches an Indian "encampment" [August 13, 1805]. The Shoshone fear an "ambuscade" [August 15, 1805]. Cameahwait doesn't merely speak; he "vociforates" [August 13, 1805]. Lewis alone uses such words as "sumptuously" [March 20, 1806], "supenemary [i.e., supernumerary]" [June 10, 1806], "disencumbered" [April 22, 1806], and "retrograde" [June 17, 1806]. Among the Shoshone Lewis has a "tolerable sound night's repose" [August 13, 1805]. Columbia Indians show "insolence" when they throw rocks at his men [April 11, 1806]. When Drewyer is caught alone by Blackfeet warriors, Lewis fears that "he would most probably fall a sacrefice"

It was Lewis, not Clark, who wrote the special orders for the Corps issued on January 1, 1806 at Fort Clatsop. The orders outline the procedures for the men to follow in dealing with Indian visitors to the fort. After detailing exactly who will be admitted under what conditions, the orders give specific instructions about how to act once an Indian visitor is inside the fort: "The Commanding Officers require and charge the Garrison to treat the natives in a friendly manner; nor will they be permitted at any time, to abuse, assault or strike them; unless such abuse assault or stroke be first given by the natives. nevertheless it shall be right for any individual, in a peaceable manner, to refuse admittance to, or put out of his room, any native who may become troublesome to him; and should such native refuse to go when requested, or attempt to enter their rooms after being forbidden to do so; it shall be the duty of the Sergeant of the guard on information of the same, to put such native out of the fort and see that he is not again admitted during the day unless specially permitted; and the Sergeant of the guard may for this purpose imploy such coercive measure (not extending to the taking of life) as shall at his discretion be deemed necessary to effect the same."[28]

[July 26, 1806]. Clark's language is thoroughly Anglo-Saxon, Lewis's heavily Latinate. Thus in the Columbia basin he writes, "my friend Capt. C. is their favorite phisician and has already received many applications. in our present situation I think it pardonable to continue this deseption for they will not give us any provision without compensation in merchandize and our stock is now reduced to a mere handfull" [May 5, 1806]. Lewis wishes to avoid the Blackfeet because "they are a vicious lawless and reather an abandoned set of wretches" [July 17, 1806]. Lewis often violates Jefferson's dictum: " . . . the most valuable of all talents is that of never using two words when one will do."[29]

It is clear that Meriwether Lewis was a more formal and admittedly less successful Indian speech writer than his patron, Thomas Jefferson.On August 3, 1803, Lewis delivered a formal address to leaders of the Oto Indians assembled beneath an awning on the banks of the Missouri River near present-day Council Bluffs, Iowa. This was Meriwether Lewis's first major Indian address. Lewis had written out the 2500-word speech, which, of course, had to be translated line by line by members of his Expedition. The following day, it was sent as a letter to the Oto absent main chief, Little Thief, and all of his people. Lewis begins, "Children. *Convene from among you the old men of experience; the men, on the wisdom of whose judgement you are willing to risk the future happiness of your nations; and the warriors, to the strength of whose arms you have been taught to look for protection in the days of danger. When in Council tranquilly assembled, reflect on the time past, and that to come; do not deceive yourselves, nor suffer others to deceive you; but like men and warriors devoted to the real interests of their nation, seek those truths; which can alone perpetuate its happiness."*

— Lewis and Clark to the Oto Indians, 4 August, 1804 (Jackson, vol. 1, p. 203).

The long letter was co-signed by William Clark. In his summary of the speech in his journal entry of August 3, 1804, Clark writes, "after Delivering a Speech informing thos Children of ours of the Change which had taken place, the wishes of our government to Cultivate friendship & good understanding, the method of have good advice & Some Directions, we made <8> 1 Great Chief to the who was not present, to whom we adresed the Speech & Sent Some presents or Meadels & flag. . . *" [August 3, 1804].*

The Riddle of Human Sexuality

Sexuality inspired a kind of strange, sometimes disturbing humor in Meriwether Lewis. Even in his earliest letters Lewis's attitudes towards sexuality seem both odd and slightly unhealthy. In a letter to his mother on October 4, 1794, for example, Lewis, just twenty years old, concludes with, "Remember me to all the girls and tell them that they must give me joy today, as I am to be married to the heaviest musquit [musket] in the Magazun tomorrow."[30] On April 6, 1795, he writes: "Remember me to Aunt and uncle Thomson and all the girls, and tell them that I shall bring an Insergiant [i.e. insurgent — presumably there are no Freudian slips in Lewis's orthography] girl to see them next fall bearing the title of Mrs. Lewis."[31] At the time of this letter, Lewis was serving in the army to put down the Whiskey Rebellion. Whether he is serious or not, he is hinting that he will marry a woman from the ranks of the rebels. He didn't.

Just inside what is now Montana, Lewis explains that "the curiossity of our party is pretty well satisfyed with rispect to" the grizzly bear, whose ferocity the Expedition had underestimated. Even though Lewis admits that the grizzlies have "staggered the resolution" of his men, he cannot refer to the sexual activities of the bears without smirking: "I expect these gentlemen will give us some amusement shotly as they soon begin now to coppolate" [May 6, 1805]. This is either prurience, or an understanding that there is something innately ridiculous in the business of mating — or both. Lewis's anthropomorphism, at least, is understandable. The linkage of bears and humans in the world's collective unconscious is as old as Homer — older.[32]

At Fort Clatsop Lewis treats Silas Goodrich for a sexually transmitted disease (STD). Somehow he finds it amusing: "Goodrich has recovered from the Louis veneri which he contracted from an amorous contact with a Chinnook damsel" [January 27, 1806]. Part of the humor seems to be in attaching a word from literary romance to an aborigine with an STD.

Still at Fort Clatsop, Lewis reports that "we were visited this afternoon by Delashshelwilt a Chinook Chief his wife and six women of his nation which the old baud his wife had brought for market. this was the same party that had communicated the venerial to so many of our party in November last, and of which they have finally recovered" [March 15,1806]. It is not quite clear just what Lewis finds funny in this, but there is a kind of patronizing humor here, based perhaps on the ludicrousness of "savages" setting up a house of prostitution. Or perhaps he is amused by the thought that the sexual urges of his men are so powerful that they are all-too-willing to risk venereal infection in a world where there is no adequate cure.

Among the Shoshone, in an otherwise straightforward excursus into ethnology, Lewis injects a slight comic edge when he discusses sexual relations. "the chastity of their women," he writes, "is not held in high estimation, and the husband will for a trifle barter the companion of his bead for a night or longer. . . ." It is the phrase "companion of his bead [i.e., bed]" that evokes the comic note. Lewis looks at Indian sexual culture through the eyes of Joseph Fielding or Restoration comedy. A moment later Lewis is astonished to report that Indian sexual codes are almost as civilized as his own. "strange as it may seem," he writes, secret adultery among the

Shoshone "... is considered as disgracefull to the husband as clandestine connections of a similar kind are among civilized nations" [August 19, 1805]. As this passage makes clear, Lewis places Indian cultures far down the hierarchy of civilization. In the same journal entry Lewis characterizes white-Indian sexual relations as a "mutual exchange of good officies," which cannot be prevented since "some months abstanence have made [the men, but not, of course, himself] very polite to those tawney damsels." Indian women are always "tawney." All are available "for market."

Lewis somehow finds time to speculate on the conundrum of the origin of venereal disease among the Indians — a debate that continues into the twenty-first century. "gonaroehah and Louis venerae" are probably "native disorders of America" [August 19, 1805], he argues, since the two diseases are common among the Shoshone, who have never before met with white people. Lewis does not stop to reflect that sex travels faster than white explorers and that — whatever else is true — his own "very polite" men are almost certainly passing on *their* STDs to Shoshone women. The medicine chest of the Corps contained mercury but not sheepskin condoms. A number of members of the Expedition had contracted venereal diseases before or during the Mandan winter interlude, and the best early nineteenth-century medicine could do was to suppress the pox, not cure it. Although Captain Lewis worries about the debilitating impact of venereal disease on his men, he nowhere expresses concern that his men may be degrading the health of the tribes through which they pass, tribes that lacked even the primitive treatments of Captain Lewis's medicine chest.

When Lewis describes Shoshone material culture — their flint knives and arrow points, or their buffalo hide shields — his prose is respectful, even at times admiring. But when he turns to their customs, what Alexis de Tocqueville would call their "habits of the heart,"[33] he exhibits an irrepressible cultural arrogance. He cannot discuss sexual relations without a smirk.

After the Expedition, when the newly-married Clark wrote to Lewis in St. Louis announcing that he would be arriving soon with his "goods" and "merchandize," Lewis deliberately misread Clark's mention of his luggage as a reference to Julia Hancock: "I must halt here in the middle of my communications and ask you if the matrimonial dictionary affords no term more appropriate than that of *goods*, alise *merchandize*, for that dear and interesting part of the creation? It is very well Genl., I shall tell madam of your want of Gallantry. . . ."[34] If William Clark ever owned a dictionary, he seldom consulted it.[35] It is not hard to detect, behind Lewis's show of gallantry, considerable unease about Clark's success in matrimony.

By now, having offered love to more than half a dozen women, all without success, Lewis joked that he was nothing more than a "fusty, rusty old bachelor." He would remain in that state until his death. After courting a certain "Miss A-n R---sh" who proved to be previously engaged, Lewis announces to his old friend Mahlon Dickerson that he is "now a perfect widower with respect to love."[36] And then the characteristic melancholia: "Thus, floating on the surface of occasion, I feel all that restlessness, that inquietude, that certain indescribable something common to old bachelors, which I cannot avoid thinking, my dear fellow, proceeds from that void in our hearts which might, or ought, to be better filled. Whence it comes, I know not, but certain it is that I never felt less like a hero than at the present moment. What may be my next adventure, God knows, but on this I am determined, to get a wife."[37] I doubt that Lewis would have used this language in a letter to William Clark. We arrange our friendships according to what they enable us to express — or explore.

Lewis's sentence, "Whence it comes, I know not, but certain it is that I never felt less like a hero than at the present moment," is extraordinarily revealing. It should be clear by now that Meriwether Lewis had a fragile ego structure. Although he is careful in this letter to avoid tying his sense of deflation solely to his mating problems, it is nevertheless the case that Lewis clearly believes that one reward for his great achievement should be success with women. The hero gets the damsel. She is never tawny. Why should the discoverer of the Great Falls of the Missouri be a fusty bachelor? The mystery of Lewis's failure in love has never been resolved.

Shortly after Clark named a beautiful stream in Montana the Judith in honor of his friend and future wife Julia Hancock [they were married January 5, 1808], Lewis, not to be outdone by his co-commander, determined to name a less beautiful river for his cousin Maria Wood. Lewis wrote:

> I determined to give it a name and in honour of Miss Maria W—d. called it Maria's River. it is true that the hue of the waters of this turbulent and troubled stream but illy comport with the pure celestial virtues and amiable qualifications of that lovely fair one; but on the other hand it is a noble river; one destined to become in my opinion an object of contention between the two great powers of America and Great Britin with rispect to the adjustment of the North westwardly boundary of the former; and that it will become one of the most interesting brances of the Missouri in a commercial point of view, I have but little doubt, as it abounds with anamals of the fur kind, and most probably furnishes a safe and direct communication to that productive country of valuable furs exclusively enjoyed at present by the subjects of his Britanic Majesty; in adition to which it passes through a rich fertile and one of the most beatifully picteresque countries that I ever beheld, through the wide expance of which, innumerable herds of living anamals are seen, it's borders garnished with one continued garden of roses, while it's lofty and open forrests, are the habitation of miriads of the feathered tribes who salute the ear of the passing traveler with their wild and simple, yet s[w]eet and cheerfull melody [June 8,1805].

There is a "miriad" of material for a psychoanalyst here. In Lewis's reasoning, the "turbulent and troubled" Marias River may not physically match the "pure celestial virtues" of Maria Wood, but it is remarkable nevertheless for its geopolitical importance. Just how the river's status as an "object of contention" between Britain and the United States resonates with Ms. Wood is not clear. Given Lewis's later difficulties in finding a wife, it is hard not to extrapolate from this description the idea that "contention" was a central fact of Meriwether Lewis's mating rites. The analogy seems to depend more on the tributary's potential commercial importance than its likelihood of creating a geopolitical and possibly military struggle between Britain and America. The Marias, Lewis argues, will also be an important source of beaver for American trappers. And if the river is not itself beautiful, Lewis assures his readers that "it passes through a rich fertile and one of the most beatifully picteresque countries that I ever beheld" [June 8, 1805].

It is not clear that Maria Wood would consider this passage an adequate tribute to her "pure celestial virtues." To anyone with even a slight acquaintance with psychoanalytic literature, it suggests sexual ambivalence and a sexual identity that is somewhat off its center of gravity.

Whatever else is true, it is certain that William Clark's naming of the Judith is heartfelt and natural, Lewis's naming of the Marias forced.

The oddity of Meriwether Lewis's sexual persona is even more in evidence on the Pacific Coast when he observes the negligent clothing style of coastal women. He writes, "when this vest is woarn the breast of the woman is concealed, but without it which is almost always the case, they are exposed, and from the habit of remaining loose and unsuspended grow to great length particularly in aged women in many of whom I have seen the bubby reach as low as the waist. The garment which occupys the waist, and from thence as low as nearly to the knee before and the ham, behind, cannot properly be denominated a petticoat, in the common acceptation of that term. . . . the whole being of sufficient thickness when the female stands erect to conceal those parts usually covered from formiliar view, but when she stoops or places herself in many other attitudes, this battery of Venus is not altogether impervious to the inquisitive and penetrating eye of the amorite" [March 19, 1806].

It is important to remember, of course, that if the journal entries tell the truth, by this time neither Meriwether Lewis nor William Clark had had sexual relations for more than two years. Perhaps any young man so deprived of sexual contact would develop, in the presence of largely naked aborigines, "the inquisitive and penetrating eye of the amorite," but not everyone would include such a revelation in his journal. There is, moreover, a strange humor at work here, which is easier to point to than analyze. Lewis confesses that observing the sexual organs of Indian women is not inadvertent. When he writes that their "battery of Venus is not altogether impervious" to his sight, he is, of course, admitting that he had to strain to catch a glimpse of the Indian women's pudenda. Pudenda which he then finds repulsive. "I think," he writes, "the most disgusting sight I have ever beheld is these dirty naked wenches" [March 19, 1806]. Meriwether Lewis was a complicated and fastidious man. No doubt Freud would say he was merely a man.

When Clark writes about sexuality, there is none of this smug prurience. At Fort Mandan, for example, without a hint of humor, he describes a love triangle involving a Mandan man, his "squar," and Sergeant Ordway. In fact, Clark's concern about the implications of the incident is unmistakable. "We derected the Serjeant Odway to give the man Some articles, at which time I told the Indian that I believed not one man of the party had touched his wife except the one he had given the use of her for a nite, in his own bed. . ." [November 22, 1804]. Unfortunately, we do not have Meriwether Lewis's description of this incident. Lewis would have been more likely to speak of "tawny damsels," "bawds," "good offices," and "companions of the bead," and he would almost certainly have cast this story into the framework of a bedroom farce.

When he describes Nez Percé clothing, Clark matter of factly notes that "The men expose those parts which are generally kept from few [view] by other nations but the women are more particular than any other nation which I have passed" [October 10, 1805]. In the hands of Meriwether Lewis this would have been all bubbies and amorities.

Summing up the condition of the men at the end of the winter at Fort Mandan, Clark writes, "Generally healthy except venerials complains which is verry Commion. . . . " [March 31, 1805]. Nothing more.

When Clark writes about the Mandan's Buffalo Medicine Dance, in which hunting skill is passed from old men . . . to young wives . . . to their young husbands by way of sexual intercourse, he declines a superb opportunity for prurience or humor. Clark merely writes that once the young man has persuaded the elder to participate, "the Girl then takes the Old man (who verry often can Screcely walk) and leades him to a Convenient place for the business, after which they return to the lodge" [January 5, 1805]. When Nicholas Biddle paraphrased Clark's matter-of-fact account of this remarkable fertility rite in the 1814 edition of the journals, he chastely employed Latin — on the sound, if puritanical, principle that anyone who could read Latin was mature enough to hear about such behavior and anyone too immature to digest such information responsibly would probably not know Latin. It is strange and even troubling to realize that Meriwether Lewis might not have passed the Biddle test on either score.

The "Biddlized" version of Clark's journal entry of January 5, 1805 reads, "Mox senex vir simulacrum parvae puellae ostensit. Tunc egrediens coetu, jecit effigium solo et superincumbens, senili ardore veneris complexit. Hoc est signum. Denique uxor e turba recessit, et jactu corporis, fovet amplexus viri solo recubante. Maritus appropinquans senex vir dejecto vultu, et honorem et dignitatem ejus conservare amplexu uxoris illum oravit. Forsitan imprimis ille refellit; dehinc, maritus multis precibus, multis lacrymis, et multis donis vehementer intercessit. Tunc senex amator perculsus misericordia, tot precibus, tot lacrymis, et tot donis, conjugali amplexu submisit. Multum ille jactatus est, sed debilis et effoetus senectute, frustra jactatus est. Maritus interdum, stans juxta, gaudet multum honore, et ejus dignitate sic conservata. Unus nostrum sodalium, multum alacrior et poetentior juventute, hac nocte honorem quatuor maritorum custodivit."[38]

Amour propre

Meriwether Lewis took himself very seriously indeed. Clark had it right when, on learning of Lewis's suicide on the Natchez Trace, wrote, "I fear O' I fear the weight of his mind has overcome him. . . ."[39]

At the end of the Mandan winter, Lewis sends a treasure of artifacts and reports to his mentor Thomas Jefferson — and, finally, financial vouchers that should have been dispatched before leaving St. Louis. The vouchers are approximately a year late. He starts by making a rather lame excuse: since he had decided not to send back a pirogue from the mouth of the Platte River (August 1804), he could not therefore forward the vouchers. He does not attempt to explain why he had not sent them from St. Louis, *before* embarking on his wilderness adventure. Lewis admits that his dilatoriness has become "a serious source of disquiet and anxiety; and the recollection of your particular charge to me on this subject, has made it still more poignant."[40] This moment is interesting partly because it is early evidence that Meriwether Lewis could not bring himself to perform certain tasks. By 1808-09 the nightmare of his official finances would become one of the primary factors contributing to his breakdown and death. Lewis's letter to the President suggests that the fatal disorganization did not creep up on him in the last difficult year of his life. It was a feature of his character. In the spring of 1805 we already see procrastination. Already we see excuses. Already guilt.

It is also interesting to notice how unhappy it made Lewis to disappoint Thomas Jefferson. He would disappoint his great patron much more profoundly in the last two years of his life. If a few dilatory financial records produced "serious . . . disquiet and anxiety," imagine what Lewis must have felt when — month after month, year after year — he failed to produce the book that would be a source of glory to himself, the President, and the nation, a book that would delight and impress Mr. Jefferson's Enlightenment friends throughout the world, a book that would establish Lewis's reputation as a serious natural scientist, a book that would quiet Federalist critics, a book that would help establish America's claims to the Northwest, a book that might possibly bring Meriwether Lewis fortune, and help him get a wife. In his letter to the President of March 10, 1801, accepting the position of secretary, Lewis made a wild promise. "Rest assured," he wrote, "I shall not relax in my exertions." But he did relax, particularly after returning from the Missouri country at the end of 1806. So far as we can tell Lewis never wrote a single page of his proposed three-volume narrative of the Expedition. Everything would come to pivot on the book. And Meriwether Lewis could not write it. And he could not admit that he could not write it.

When Lewis was offered his position as Thomas Jefferson's secretary in the spring of 1801, he wrote a revealingly triumphant letter to his friend Ferdinand Claiborne on March 7th:[41]

> I cannot withhold from you my friend the agreeable intelligence I received on my arrival at this place by way of a very polite note from Thomas Jefferson, the newly elected President of the United States, signifying his wish that I should except the office of his private Secretary;

So far so good. Now Lewis begins to puff himself up:

> this unbounded confidence, conferred on me by a man whose virtue and talents I have ever adored, and always conceived second to none, I must confess did not fail to raise me somewhat in

> my own estimation, insomuch that I have almost prevailed on myself to believe that my abilities are equal to the task.

"Unbounded confidence"? "Adored"? Jefferson's confidence was no doubt considerable, but nothing in his letter of February 23, 1801 suggests that it was unbounded. Lewis flatters himself. And he directly declares that his sense of self-worth is tied to the opinion of others. Jefferson's regard has "raised me somewhat in my own estimation." Apparently Lewis has not been reading his self-help literature. At the end of his letter Lewis rather pompously informs Claiborne that "I shal take the liberty of informing you of the most important political occurrences of our government or such of them as I may feel myself at liberty to give." Lewis writes as if he has just been appointed Secretary of State.

Compare this self-regard to the sensibility of Lewis's partner in discovery. When William Clark accepted Lewis's offer (made by letter, June 19, 1803) to accompany him up the Missouri, Clark wrote, "I will cheerfully join you my friend" [July 18, 1803]. Such was Clark. But Lewis in his reply to this letter puffed himself into Ciceronian prose. On August 3, 1803 he wrote, "I could neither hope, wish, nor expect from a union with any man on earth more perfect support or further aid in the discharge of the several duties of my mission than that which, I am confident, I shall derive from being associated with yourself." The Expedition is now a mission.

Lewis's journal entries return to four basic themes again and again: **first**, that he is going where no civilized man has gone before; **second**, that he has dreamed of exploring the Missouri country for much of his life; **third**, that he needs to succeed as if his life depended upon it; and **fourth**, that any significant setback might bring about the failure of the Expedition.

By this standard, William Clark was a happy-go-lucky man.

The first civilized man

Meriwether Lewis never felt so much like Columbus as when he was leaving Fort Mandan, the last outpost of European presence on the Missouri. The date was April 7, 1805. He believed he was passing from a relatively well-known country into *terra incognita*. A few days later (April 14, 1805) Lewis declares that the Expedition had now reached "the highest point to which any whiteman had ever ascended." And yet in the same sentence — as if anticipating the eventual erosion of his claims to "discovery" in American historiography — Lewis immediately adds, "except two Frenchmen . . . who having lost their way had straggled a few miles further, tho' to what place precisely I could not learn.—" These small concessions aside, the true discovery phase of the Expedition was about to begin, and Lewis was fully alive to the magnitude of the moment. He could not be content, on this occasion, to jot down field notes. He strained for the heroic. In the middle of what would become North Dakota, he indited epic prose:

> Our vessels consisted of six small canoes, and two large perogues. This little fleet altho' not quite so rispectable as those of Columbus or Capt. Cook, were still viewed by us with as much pleasure as those deservedly famed adventurers ever beheld theirs; and I dare say with quite as much anxiety for their safety and preservation. we were now about to penetrate a country at least two thousand miles in width, on which the foot of civilized man had never trodden; the good or evil it had in store for us was for experiment to determine, and these little vessells contained every article by which we were to expect to subsist or defend ourselves. [April 7, 1805]

Lewis's desire to become a "deservedly famed adventurer" is unmistakable. His heroic imagination has transformed a few crude boats into a little fleet. In his mind's eye he pictures Columbus alone at Palos in southern Spain, on the eve of his departure (August 2, 1492), silently (and alone) surveying his little fleet. Lewis's claim to be the first civilized man to tread on a two thousand mile quadrant from North Dakota to the Pacific Coast is splendid, if untrue in the particular sense in which he means the term, and of course it begs the question of just what the "foot of civilized man" looks like.

Two months later, at the Great Falls of the Missouri, five hundred miles deeper into the heart of darkness, a disconsolate Lewis wishes that he were an artist or a poet so that "I might be enabled to give to the enlightened world some just idea of this truly magnifficent and sublimely grand object, which has from the commencement of time been concealed from the view of civilized man" [June 13, 1805]. The grandeur of the Great Falls is less important than the fact that nobody worth mentioning has ever been there before.

In the vicinity of the Three Forks, when Sacagawea "recognizes the country and assures us that this is the river on which her relations live," Lewis writes that "this peice of information has cheered the sperits of the party who now begin to console themselves with the anticipation of shortly seeing the head of the missouri yet unknown to the civilized world" [July 22, 1805]. If it is true that Meriwether Lewis was a manic depressive, in an age when painkillers and psychotropic drugs came mainly in the form of grain alcohol, Lewis may have employed the Columbian pose, the proclamation of mission, the sense of heroic purpose, to keep himself in motion.

Dreaming of exploring the Missouri most of his life . . .

Twice Lewis informs us that he has dreamed of exploring the Missouri River for much of his life. Leaving Fort Mandan on April 7, 1805, he writes of the Expedition as "a voyage which had formed a da[r]ling project of mine for the last ten years. . . . I could," he writes, "but esteem this moment of my <our> departure as among the most happy of my life." This passage comes at the start of what Lewis conceived of as the unprecedented part of the Expedition. Up until now, it is clear, Lewis believed he has been threading his way through relatively well-known territory. In the mind of the commander, the lower Missouri, from St. Louis to Fort Mandan, is blasé. It is possible that he was not assiduous about his journal between May 14, 1804 and April 7, 1805 because he considered the first year of travel to be a kind of shakedown cruise through familiar land. In the lower Missouri, there was plenty of country to get through, but not much to discover. West of Fort Mandan is *terra incognita*. Suddenly Lewis, the journalist, comes back to life in a big way. Meriwether Lewis is an excellent starter, but he tends always to finish badly.

At the other end of the Missouri River, at its putative source near Lemhi Pass, Lewis declares that "the road took us to the most distant fountain of the waters of the mighty Missouri in surch of which we have spent so many toilsome days and wristless nights. thus far I had accomplished one of those grand objects on which my mind has been unalterably fixed for many years" [August 12, 1805]. He has reached his goal. He has explored the Missouri River from its mouth to its source. Until now the fountain of the Missouri River has been shrouded in mystery. Heraclitus[42] notwithstanding, it is like one of those prostrate redwoods with the dates of the Great Wall of China, the Crusades, and the penning of *Hamlet* marked on its concentric rings. Now the source of the Missouri River has at last been pinpointed on the map of North America. Lewis has dragged boats across a continent. Not even the appalling view westward from Lemhi Pass could destroy Lewis's sense of triumph. One can hear the first draft of the autobiography of Meriwether Lewis here.

We know from Jefferson himself that Lewis was not exaggerating when he said he had wanted to explore the Missouri River "for many years." In his 1814 biographical sketch of his neighbor and secretary, Jefferson explains that Lewis had applied to him to accompany Andre Michaux on his (abortive) 1793 expedition up the Missouri River, sponsored by the American Philosophical Society. Jefferson wrote that the eighteen-year-old Lewis "warmly solicited me to obtain for him the execution of that object [a place in the proposed expedition]."[43] Jefferson had then explained to Lewis that Michaux would be traveling with a single — and older — companion. Ten years later, when Jefferson finally mounted an expedition during the first term of his presidency, he remembered both the capacities and the enthusiasm of his young neighbor. Cast your bread upon the waters.

Needing to succeed as if his life depended upon it . . .

Again and again Lewis declares that he equates the success of his Expedition not merely with his reputation but with his life.

In eastern Montana, when Charbonneau for the second time nearly sank the white pirogue, Lewis, who was watching helplessly on shore three hundred yards away, briefly contemplated trying to swim to the stricken vessel. In retrospect, he admitted that to have attempted to swim the cold and swift Missouri would have cost him his life: "had I undertaken this project therefore, there was a hundred to one but what I should have paid the forfit of my life for the madness of my project, but this had the perogue been lost, I should have valued but little—" [May 14, 1805]. Undoubtedly the loss of the pirogue would have been a serious blow to the Expedition, but it is unlikely that the Corps of Discovery would have collapsed so long as sufficient rifles and powder remained. Lewis exaggerated the fragility of one of the most resourceful teams ever assembled.

Later that summer, among the Shoshone, he writes: "I slept but little as might be well expected, my mind dwelling on the state of the expedition which I have ever held in equal estimation with my own existence" [August 16, 1805].

This is taking things rather too seriously, even for the commander of a pathfinding mission into the American West. If Lewis's life would not be worth living after a boat accident that was out of his control, imagine how he must have punished himself for not writing a book that he had it entirely in his power to produce.

Contemplating failure at any significant setback . . .

Whenever things reach a critical stage, Lewis contemplates failure.

The first geographical crisis came at the confluence of the Marias and the Missouri on June 3, 1805. The captains were not expecting a major northern tributary. After they came to terms with their initial sense of puzzlement,

Lewis and Clark decided that the northern fork must be the tributary, the southern fork the true Missouri. Their read of the landscape was so far from being obvious that every other member of the Expedition, including the indispensable Drewyer, declared that the north fork was the true Missouri. Each captain led a reconnaissance team to learn more. Lewis was clearly anxious. "to mistake the stream at this period of the season," he wrote, "two months of the traveling season having now elapsed, and to ascend such stream to the rocky Mountain or perhaps much further before we could inform ourselves whether it did approach the Columbia or not, and then be obliged to return and take the other stream would not only loose us the whole of this season but would probably so dishearten the party that it might defeat the expedition altogether" [June 3, 1805]. The captains were right, the men wrong. Their credibility must have soared in the wake of this masterful trailblazing.

Two months later the Expedition entered another critical phase. From their winter conversations with the Hidatsa in North Dakota, Lewis and Clark knew that would almost certainly need horses to cross the Rocky Mountains, and that the horse people nearest to the source of the Missouri River were the Shoshone, who could be expected to be elusive because of their fears of attack by gun-toting plains Indians. When an encounter with the Shoshone did not occur as early as he had estimated, Lewis began to panic. "we begin to feel considerable anxiety with rispect to the Snake Indains." he wrote. "if we do not find them or some other nation who have horses I fear the successfull issue of our voyage will be very doubtfull or at all events much more difficult in it's accomplishment" [July 27, 1805].

The Shoshone proved to be even more timorous than the captains had anticipated. During the four days that he spent more or less alone with the tribe, before the coming of Clark and Sacagawea, Lewis was perfectly aware that he could not afford for his early negotiations with the Shoshone to collapse: "I knew that if these people left me that they would immediately disperse and secrete themselves in the mountains where it would be impossible to find them or at least in vain to pursue them and that they would spread the allarm to all other bands within our reach & of course we should be disappointed in obtaining horses, which would vastly retard and increase the labour of our voyage and I feared might so discourage the men as to defeat the expedition altogether" [August 16, 1805]. It's the old refrain. Lewis might have ended his sentence at "increase the labour of our voyage." There is no evidence in the journals that the men of the Corps of Discovery ever actually became seriously discouraged. Either the state of the Expedition was more fragile than we know or Meriwether Lewis is exaggerating.

Still among the Shoshone when he realizes that the Bitterroot transit must be made by horses, Lewis writes, " . . . I directed the fiddle to be played and the party danced very merily much to the amusement and gratification of the natives, though I must confess that the state of my own mind at this moment did not well accord with the prevailing mirth as I somewhat feared that the caprice of the indians might suddenly induce them to withhold their horses from us without which my hopes of prosicuting my voyage to advantage was lost" [August 26, 1805].

The silhoutte at the right is signed by and attributed to Dolley Madison, wife of Jefferson protégé and fourth United States president, James Madison. She may have done Lewis's silhoutte while serving as the unofficial First Lady during widower Jefferson's presidency. Strikingly similar in outline to the least-known image of Lewis by Saint-Mémin (bottom, page 11), it may be the work of silhouettist Uri Hill, who visited Washington in June 1803. Dolley Madison may have simply owned the silhoutte done by Hill. See Ellen G. Miles, Saint-Mémin and the Neoclassical Profile Portrait in America, *p. 339.*

Co-Captains

Lewis called William Clark co-captain and insisted, at the end of the journey, that his partner be granted equal monetary rewards and land grants, but it is clear from the journals that Lewis took command at critical moments in the Expedition. He seems to have wanted to make the great discoveries of the Expedition alone. Thus on the western border of what is now North Dakota, Lewis left Clark behind and pressed on with a small group of men to the confluence of the Missouri and Yellowstone rivers. His ostensible justification for thus anticipating the rest of the company was to get a head start on determining the longitude and latitude of so strategic a place in the northwest. Only after he had made his celestial observations and reflected alone about the importance of the great confluence did Lewis walk down and join "the party at their encampment on the point of land fromed by the junction of the rivers" [April 26, 1805]. Characteristically, while Lewis philosophizes, William Clark takes on

Lewis wrote to President Jefferson at the end of the Expedition: "With rispect to the exertions and services rendered by that esteemable man Capt. William Clark in the course of late voyage I cannot say too much; if sir any credit be due for the success of the arduous enterprize in which we have been mutually engaged, he is equally with myself entitled to your consideration and that of our common country." — Lewis to Jefferson, September 23, 1806 the more mundane role of measuring the rivers: " . . . the bed of the Missouri 520 yards wide. . . the yellowstone river . . . 858 yds." [April 26, 1805].

Similarly Lewis made sure he was the first "civilized man" to see the Great Falls of the Missouri River on June 13, 1805. This time the rationale was that he must press ahead to the falls to confirm that the Corps of Discovery was ascending the correct branch of the Missouri River. Everyone except the captains had declared the Marias to be the mainstem, and Lewis was genuinely concerned to confirm his geographical hunch and alleviate the men's concerns about the route. But Clark might easily have become the "first civilized man" to see the Great Falls of the Missouri. Lewis insisted upon striking out ahead of the party in spite of the fact that he was at the time suffering from a digestive ailment. Just before he set out he reported that "I felt myself very unwell this morning and took a portion of salts from which I feel much relief." Lewis's rationale? "this expedition I prefered undertaking as Capt. C. best waterman &c" [June 9, 1805]. Clark's role was to move the flotilla up river. Lewis, like Huck Finn, preferred to light out ahead of the rest. Clark's mastery as a waterman must at times have felt like a form of confinement.

A month later, Lewis became the first member of the Corps to see the source of the Missouri in what is now southwestern Montana, and the first to drink from waters of the Columbia basin in what is now Idaho. He has no choice in the journals but to acknowledge that he was not utterly alone, but he goes out of his way to ridicule Hugh McNeal's role in the drama. " . . . two miles below," he writes, "McNeal had exultingly stood with a foot on each side of this little rivulet [what Lewis took to be the source of the Missouri][44] and thanked his god that he had lived to bestride the mighty & heretofore deemed endless Missouri" [August 12, 1805]. When Lewis can think of nothing else by way of belittlement, he calls someone a Catholic. It is not that he wants to dismiss McNeal. He merely intends to subordinate him. Columbus always surveys the New World alone.

On the one occasion when Clark insisted on being the Expedition's pathfinder, circumstance thwarted his will. In southwestern Montana, Clark determined to make the initial contact with the Shoshone Indians himself, perhaps because he was already more intimate than Lewis with Sacagawea, who had been brought along for precisely this encounter, perhaps because he had a higher tolerance for Indian ways than his partner in discovery, perhaps because he wanted to do a little pathfinding himself for a change.

Unfortunately, Clark's reconnaissance proved to be premature by several hundred miles. He embarked from the Gates of the Mountains (near present Helena, Montana), unaware that the Shoshones lived far up the Jefferson River, weeks beyond the Three Forks of the Missouri, which the Expedition had not yet reached. Clark set out on July 19, 1805. The Corps of Discovery did not finally make contact with the Shoshone until August 13. To make matters worse, Clark's feet became so seriously infected on his march that he had to desist. Meriwether Lewis reasserted his primacy just in time to secure the Shoshone "discovery" for himself.

Just what Clark thought of all of this goes largely unreported, but it is clear that he was deeply disappointed, and it is possible that he was annoyed. He grumps in his diary, "I Should have taken this trip had I have been able to march" [August 9, 1805]. Lewis was clearly aware that it was Columbus and not his crew, Captain Cook and not his mates who were remembered by history. The challenge for Lewis was to make sure he played the role of primary discoverer without ever having to pull rank on his friend. Lewis had to invent rationalizations for pressing on ahead without overtly revealing the ambitions that drove him to the forefront.

The artificiality of this *modus operandi* reveals itself in the Shoshone encounter. When Lewis finally made contact with these critically-important horsemen, he was without Sacagawea — the Shoshone interpreter brought along on the Voyage of Discovery for precisely this encounter! By now Sacagawea swam in Clark's orbit, not Lewis's. Clark was behind, pushing the boats up the

Beaverhead River. Lewis apparently believed that he could establish relations with the Shoshone without his Shoshone interpreter. This from a man who just two months previously had responded to Sacagawea's nearly-mortal illness by writing that she was " . . . our only dependence for a friendly negociation with the Snake Indians on whom we depend for horses to assist us in our portage from the Missouri to the columbia River" [June 16, 1805]. It turned out that Lewis was as right as he was confident — he did make successful contact with the Shoshone without the help of Sacagawea. His relations with the Shoshone were agonizingly tense, but he forged them by himself.

The irony — owing partly to Lewis's inability to publish an account of his adventures — is that William Clark is indelibly etched into the American consciousness as the equal partner in the Voyage of Discovery, in spite of Lewis's attempt to husband key moments of glory for himself. It would be very interesting to know just how he would have presented his partnership with Clark, had he lived to publish his narrative. Generous though Lewis was with respect to that "esteemable man" William Clark, it seems likely — if the journals are any indication — that Lewis would have found a range of ways to make clear to the world that *he* was the President's secretary, the leader of the Expedition, and the discoverer of the source of the Missouri River, the man of destiny, and that Clark was co-captain by virtue of Meriwether Lewis's magnanimity rather than in actual rank. Any notion of Clark's equality in the adventure would need to be seen as a manifestation of Lewis's generosity of spirit rather than an actual parity of roles. Indeed, Jefferson would probably have egged him on.

The gaps in Lewis's journal are legendary. On 702 days (of a total of 1120 from the time he began to keep a journal on August 31, 1803, to the return to St. Louis on September 23, 1806) Lewis either wrote nothing, or what he wrote has been lost.[45] Without William Clark's assiduousness as a diarist, we would have no adequate narrative of the Expedition. The only gap in Clark's journal from May 14, 1804 to the Expedition's return consists of just ten days, and on the eleventh he summarized the period he had missed. The narrative thread we have for the Lewis and Clark Expedition is essentially the work of William Clark. History belongs to those who write. Lewis should have let his muse be Amerigo Vespucci rather than Columbus. The best thing William Clark ever did for himself was to force himself every night, in sickness and in health, in flush times and lean, no matter how profound his fatigue, to keep a journal. The Journals of Lewis and Clark might justly be called a narrative by William Clark with occasional field notes and reveries by Captain Meriwether Lewis.

Unlike Clark, who is usually content to report the facts of the day, Lewis often finds time to indulge in psychological speculations. Lewis is more truly a journalist (in the Boswellian sense) than Clark. He seems genuinely interested in charting the course of his soul as well as that of the Missouri River. He seems to take a kind of pride in musing about the human condition, about the nature of happiness, even about the nature of heroism. Leaving Fort Mandan on April 7, 1805, for example, Lewis acknowledges that attitude plays as important a role as circumstance in determining one's response to events. " . . . the state of mind in which we are, generally gives the colouring to events, when the immagination is suffered to wander into futurity," he muses. Optimism, and a ten-years' anticipation of this moment, give Lewis confidence, regardless of the fact that he is "now about to penetrate a country at least two thousand miles in width, on which the foot of civilized man had never trodden," utterly dependent on the men and equipment he has assembled. In spite of the uncertainty and the dangers that lie before him, Lewis asserts that he considers "this moment of my <our> departure as among the most happy of my life."

Notice that in this pivotal moment in the Voyage of Discovery, the other thirty-some men and one woman have disappeared from Meriwether Lewis's consciousness. He writes of *my* departure and *my* life. In the mind of Captain Lewis, Nathaniel Pryor, John Ordway, Patrick Gass, William Bratton, John Colter, Joseph and

Reuben Field, John Shields, George Gibson, George Shannon, John Potts, John Collins, Joseph Whitehouse, Richard Windsor, Alexander Willard, Hugh Hall, Silas Goodrich, Robert Frazer, Pierre Cruzatte, Baptiste Lepage, François Labiche, Hugh McNeal, William Werner, Thomas P. Howard, Peter Weiser, John B. Thompson, York, George Drewer, Charbonneau and "his Indian Squar" are merely "the party." Lewis's self-absorption is nearly complete.

In a private letter written at the end of the Mandan winter, Lewis writes: "The ice in the Missouri has now nearly disappea[red]. I shal set out on my voyage in the course of a few days." It is true that this letter was written to Lewis's mother. In communication with one's mother, assertions of primacy are of course permissible, perhaps even required. Still, writing to President Jefferson at the same time, Lewis speaks of "the enterprise in which I am engaged."[46] Before signing off to the President, Lewis does speak of "my inestimable friend and companion, Captain Clark," but it is not difficult to detect a slightly patronizing attitude here, or at least *noblesse oblige*.

Later, when Lewis's always considerable ego had expanded with the fame that came from his success, he published a haughty letter in the *National Intelligencer* denouncing spurious narratives of his tour, and particularly attacking enlisted man Robert Frazer's proposed narrative. Amazingly, they remained on friendly terms. The publishing agent for Sergeant Patrick Gass issued a lengthy reply in the Pittsburgh *Gazette* on April 14, 1807 in which he sarcastically wrote, ". . . it may perhaps be agreeable to Your Excellency to know the reasons of my interfering in this affair of the journals of what you modestly call *your* late tour."[47] Lewis's haughtiness may have brought about a literary catastrophe. Robert Frazer's unpublished journal disappeared; it has not resurfaced.

President Jefferson did not help much. Famous as a collector of protégés, to whom he was unashamedly loyal, he persisted in calling the Voyage of Discovery "Mr. Lewis's tour" long after it had become clear that William Clark had played a critical role in its success, possibly even *the* critical role. The President even spoke of the famous map of the American West — exclusively Clark's achievement—as "Mr. Lewis's map."

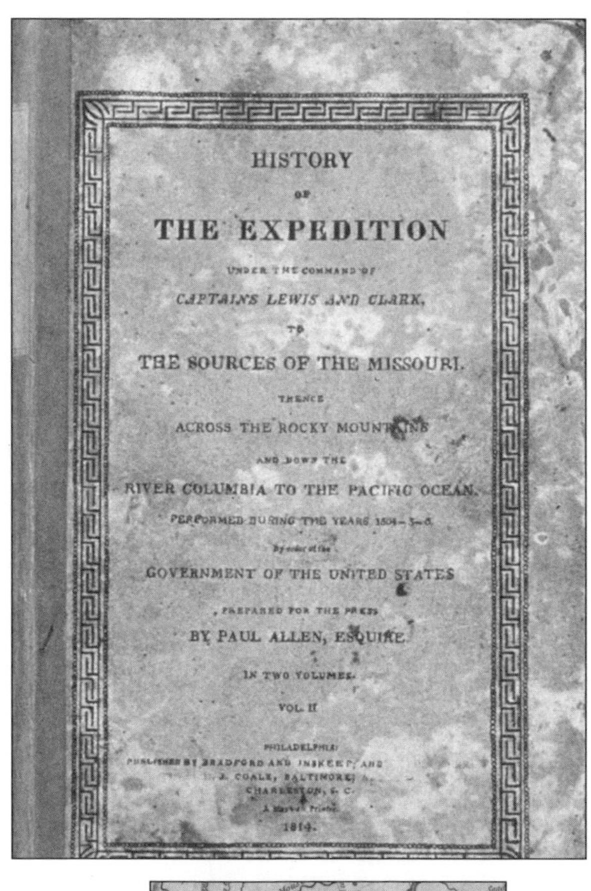

HISTORY
OF
THE EXPEDITION
UNDER THE COMMAND OF
CAPTAINS LEWIS AND CLARK,
TO
THE SOURCES OF THE MISSOURI,
THENCE
ACROSS THE ROCKY MOUNTAINS
AND DOWN THE
RIVER COLUMBIA TO THE PACIFIC OCEAN.
PERFORMED DURING THE YEARS 1804–5–6.
By order of the
GOVERNMENT OF THE UNITED STATES.
PREPARED FOR THE PRESS
BY PAUL ALLEN, ESQUIRE.
IN TWO VOLUMES.
VOL. II
PHILADELPHIA:
PUBLISHED BY BRADFORD AND INSKEEP; AND
J. COALE, BALTIMORE;
CHARLESTON, S. C.
1814.

Finally published in 1814, the History of the Expedition Under the Command of Captains Lewis and Clark *included Clark's map, copied by Samuel Lewis of Philadelphia for publication with the edition edited by Paul Allen and Nicholas Biddle. The cover in original board is from Volume II of the 1814 edition. The map detail below, featuring Fort Mandan where Lewis and Clark wintered in 1804-1805, like everything in the Expedition's map of the American West, is the achievement of William Clark, not Meriwether Lewis. Clark alone was the Expedition's cartographer.*

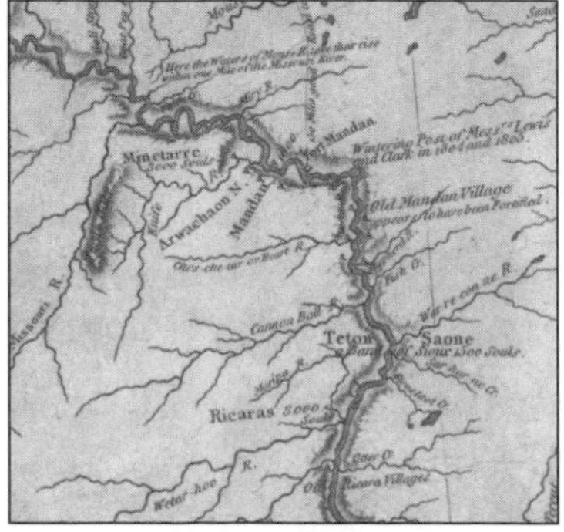

Deadly Sins: Wrath

How often did Meriwether Lewis get angry? Often, if the records we have are representative. He was angry at the inept tailor of his officer's coat (see above, page 8). He was justifiably angry at the builder of the expedition's keelboat. To Jefferson, Lewis wrote on September 8, 1803, "I had been moste shamefully detained by the unpardonable negligence of my boat-builder. . . . I threatened him with the penalty of his contract . . . I spent most of my time with the workmen, alternately persuading and threatening, but neither threats, persuasion or any other means which I could devise were sufficient to procure the completion of the work sooner. . . ."[48] He was justifiably angry when Pierre Cruzatte shot him in the buttocks in a willow thicket on the return journey ("Damn you, you have shot me"), though he calmed down remarkably quickly considering the seriousness of the accident and Cruzatte's less-than-candid explanation of why he did not respond to Lewis's repeated attempts to hail him after the bullet tore through his breeches. With almost philosophical calm he writes, "I do not believe that the fellow did it intentionally but after finding that he had shot me was anxious to conceal his knowledge of having done so" [August 11, 1806]. Perhaps he was in too much pain to exert the energy of wrath.

He was angry at both mosquitoes and himself on July 17, 1805, when he slept out without the benefit of his protective netting, and "of course suffered considerably, and promised in my wrath that I never will be guilty of a similar peice of negligence while on this voyage." He was angry at unnamed hunters who did not return at the appointed time on May 8, 1806, and thus held up the Expedition's departure: " . . . we chid them severely for their indolence and inattention to the order of last evening," Lewis writes. At the base of the Bitterroot Mountains, he was angry at Willard for permitting his horse to "ramble off." "It was not to be found," Lewis writes, " . . . when I ordered the others to be brought up and confined to the picquits. this in addition to the other difficulties under which I laboured was truly provoking. I repremanded him more severely for this peice of negligence than had been usual with me" [April 19, 1806]. Among other things, this outburst reveals that Lewis routinely issues reprimands, though at a slightly lower volume. And that Willard was the victim of accumulated stresses.

He was angry enough at a Nez Percé man who stole a socket to beat him severely on April 21, 1806 (see below, page 90).

He was angry at Charbonneau at Shoshone Cove, when the dim-witted Frenchman failed to inform him that Cameahwait and his people were preparing to abandon the Corps of Discovery in favor of their annual buffalo hunt on the Montana plains. "I was," Lewis writes, "out of patience with the folly of Charbono who had not sufficient sagacity to see the consequencies which would inevitably flow from such a movement of the indians, and altho' he had been in possession of this information since early in the morning . . . yet he never mentioned it to me untill after noon. I could not forbear speaking to him with some degree of asperity on this occasion" [August 25, 1805]. Does this mean a military rebuke or a screaming fit? In Lewis's eyes, Charbonneau was always a buffoon, and sometimes a genuine threat to the success of the Expedition. Still, he made an excellent *boudin blanc*.

One of Lewis's best outbursts was written in St. Louis before the Expedition got underway. Frustrated by his relations with the fur entrepreneurs Manuel Lisa and Francois Marie Benoit, Lewis wrote:

> Damn Manuel and triply damn Mr. B. They give me more vexation and trouble than their lives are worth. I have dealt very plainly with these gentlemen. In short, I have come to an open rupture with them. I think them both scoundrels and they have given me abundant proofs of their unfriendly disposition towards our Government and its measures. These gentlemen — no, I will scratch it out — these puppies are not unacquainted with my opinions and I am well informed that they have engaged some hireling writer to draught a petition and remonstrance to Govr. Claiborne against me. Strange, indeed, that men to appearance in their senses will manifest such strong symptoms of insanity as to whetting knives to cut their own throats.[49]

What can be said of this excursion into petulance? It is clear that Lewis does not possess his patron's famous equanimity of spirit. It is clear that he has not, like the President, mastered the stoicism of the classical philosopher Epictetus. He has none of the "artificial good humor" which Jefferson encouraged in a now-famous letter to his grandson Thomas Jefferson Randolph in 1808.[50] It is clear that Lewis had a propensity for making enemies, some of whom would do great damage to his reputation in the last years of his life. And it is sadly clear that it was Lewis himself who came to manifest tendencies — paranoia, pettiness, impatience, pride, self-pity — that led him to cut his own throat. Manuel Lisa was a scoundrel, but he understood the character of Meriwether Lewis. Lewis, he wrote, is "fond of exaggerating everything relative to his Expedition and . . . a very headstrong and, in many instances, an imprudent man."[51] Who can disagree with this assessment?

The testimony of Lewis's detractors is always similar. The British trader Charles McKenzie spent enough time with Lewis at Fort Mandan to conclude: "It is true Captain Lewis could not make himself agreeable to us. He could speak fluently and learnedly on all subjects, but his inveterate disposition against the British stained, at least in our eyes, all his eloquence."[52] It is worth remembering that Lewis's father died (November 1779) while serving in the American army during the Revolutionary War. Both Lewis and Jefferson were profound Anglophobes, but the President, unlike his protégé, virtually never failed to "make himself agreeable" to everyone. Like most of Jefferson's protégés, Lewis shares the master's attitudes, but not his preternatural gracefulness.

Lewis could not even restrain himself in an official report to the government of the United States. From Fort Mandan he wrote a venomous assessment of the Teton Sioux: "These are the vilest miscreants of the savage race and must ever remain the pirates of the Missouri until such measures are pursued by our Government as will make them feel a dependence on its will for their supply of merchandise. Unless these people are reduced to order, by coercive measures, I am ready to pronounce that the citizens of the United States can never enjoy but partially the advantages which the Missouri presents."[53] This is imperfect diplomacy, a kind of sassy reply to Thomas Jefferson's claim that "on that nation [the Sioux] we wish most particularly to make a friendly impression, because of their immense power, and because we learn they are very desirous of being on the most friendly terms with us."[54]

When Drewyer and Shields, failing to intuit the Captain's desire that they should halt, scare off a Shoshone man near the source of the Missouri, Lewis writes: "I now felt quite as much mortification and disappointment as I had pleasure and expectation at the first sight of this indian. I fet soarly chargrined at the conduct of the men particularly Sheilds to whom I principally attributed this failure in obtaining an introduction to the natives. I now called the men to me and could not forbare abraiding them a little for their want of attention, and imprudence, on this occasion" [August 11, 1805]. This is rare criticism of Drewyer, who is the one member of the Expedition who can do no wrong. And another thing! Drewyer and Shields had forgotten to bring up Lewis's telescope ("my spye-glass"), which Lewis himself "had droped in the plain." He sent them back to retrieve it. Bad day.

Out near the source of the Missouri, Patrick Gass lost one of the Expedition's pipe tomahawks. It is clear from the journals that the often-irritable Lewis wants to be angry with Gass (and probably was), but that he fights successfully on this occasion to exhibit Mr.

Jefferson's "artificial good humour." "soon after passing the river this morning Sergt. Gass lost my tommahawk in the thick brush and we were unable to find it, I regret the loss of this usefull implement, however accedents will happen in the best families, and I consoled myself with the recollection that it was not the only one we had with us" [August 2, 1805]. Gass was lucky.

Patrick M. Gass, born June 12, 1771 at Falling Springs, Pennsylvania, was a sergeant with Captain Russell Bissell's company of the First Infantry, stationed at Fort Kaskaskia in 1803 when Meriwether Lewis came down the Ohio River in search of volunteers to join the Expedition. Bissell agreed to release Sergeant John Ordway to Lewis, but he did not wish to give up the services of Gass, who was both a seasoned soldier and skilled carpenter. Lewis insisted, and Bissell relented. Enlisted as a private in the Expedition, Gass was elected sergeant by the men following the death of Sergeant Charles Floyd in August 1804. His journal, which appeared in 1807, was the first account published by any member of the Expedition. Lewis became concerned when he heard that Gass intended to publish. In an open letter to the National Intelligencer *in Washington, D.C., printed March 14, 1807, Lewis says that only Robert Frazer was authorized to publish [Frazer's journal has never been found]. Lewis warned the public about "several unauthorised and probably some spurious publications now preparing for the press, on the subject of my late tour to the Pacific Ocean by individuals entirely unknown to me, I have considered it a duty which I owe the public, as well as myself to put them on their guard with respect to such publications, lest from the practice of such impositions they may be taught to depreciate the worth of the work which I am myself preparing for publication. . . ."[55] Gass's publisher retorted with a stinging rebuke, suggesting that Lewis was attempting to reserve for himself all profit from publication of accounts of the Expedition. In fact, says publisher David McKeehan, Gass " . . . may in some respects be considered as having the advantage; for while your Excellency was star-gazing, and taking celestial observations, he was taking observations of the world below."[56]*

The Problem of Alcohol

The drinking problem began early. It is perhaps symbolically appropriate that Lewis's inheritance, in addition to 520 pounds sterling in cash, twenty-four slaves, and something less than 2000 acres of land, included 147 gallons of whiskey.[57]

In a letter to his mother Lucy Marks written from Winchester, Virginia, at the age of twenty, Lewis boasts, " We have mountains of beef and oceans of whiskey, and I feel myself able to share it with the heartiest fellow in camp." A few weeks later, on Christmas eve 1794, he admits that the meal was not much to write home about ("a little stewed beef"), but "to my great comfort I have this Day been so fortunate as for the price of one dollar to procure a quart of Rum for a chrismas dram."[58]

Whatever else it was, his court-martial in November 1795, had something to do with excessive drinking, in a profession and a time and at a place where heavy drinking was the norm. Lieutenant Elliott alleged that Lewis burst into his room "abruptly, and in an Ungentleman like manner, when intoxicated . . . and without provocation insulting him, and disturbing the peace and harmony of a Company of Officers whom he had invited there."[59] The course of human events takes some odd turns. If Lewis had not been drinking to excess, he might not have quarreled with Lieutenant Elliott. If he had not been court-martialed, he would not have been transferred to a company commanded by William Clark. If he had not met William Clark, he would presumably have chosen somebody else in 1803 to be his partner in discovery. If he had chosen someone else. . . .

There is no evidence in the journals that Meriwether Lewis drank to excess during the Expedition. No other diarist even hints at intoxication. Undoubtedly Lewis drank his portion, along with everyone else. It is true that Lewis reports on more than one occasion that the combination of fatigue, Herculean labor, and the infrequency of alcohol consumption on the Voyage of Discovery tended to transform occasional rations of whiskey into serious intoxication, but he always suggests that he is observing the phenomenon among the men, not in himself. On May 29, 1805, for example, Lewis writes: "we . . . fixed our camp and gave each man a small dram. notwithstanding the allowance of sperits we issued did not exceed ½ pn. [per] man several of them were considerably effected by it; such is the effects of abstaining for some time from the uce of sperituous liquors; they were all very merry.—"

Was there a separate supply of liquor for the officers? The sense of the journals is that no such distinction was made. It is the case, however, that we would be unlikely to be informed of an officer's stash of whiskey, much less Meriwether Lewis's secret supply. One tantalizing clue exists, thanks to the flash flood that carried away some gear and might well have cost Clark and the Charbonneau family their lives. We learn on June 29, 1805 that York is carrying a canteen of alcohol. Clark, worried about the delicate health of Sacagawea, who had been thoroughly soaked by the flash flood, offers the only medicine available to him. "I caused her," he wrote, "as also the others of the party to take a little Spirits, which my Servent had in a Canteen, which revived verry much" [June 29, 1805]. It is not clear just what this signifies, except that the control and dissemination of alcohol were probably more complicated than they seem from a cursory reading of the journals. If the slave York had whiskey at this late date, he can hardly have been the only one.

After Charbonneau nearly sank the white pirogue on May 14, 1805, and only the resolution of Pierre Cruzatte and Sacagawea prevented disaster, Lewis writes, " . . . we thought it a proper occasion to console ourselves and cheer the sperits of our men and accordingly took a drink of grog and gave each man a gill of sperits." On this occasion, at least, Lewis appears to order grog as much for himself as for his company. Note that on this occasion, at least, the captains drink from one source, the rest of the men from another.

At the time of the Biddle edition of the journals in 1814, Jefferson suggested that Meriwether Lewis's drinking problems were long-standing, that he had noticed this propensity in Lewis during the White House apprenticeship between May 1801 and the spring of 1803, and that it had become clear to Jefferson that Lewis's problem had grown worse following his return from the Missouri country. "He was much afflicted and habitually so, with hypochondria," Jefferson wrote. "This was probably increased by the habit into which he had fallen and the painful reflections that would necessarily produce in a mind like his."[60] No doubt Jefferson is telling the truth as he sees it, but it is worth keeping in mind that Jefferson was at times rather puritanical about the drinking habits of the American people,[61] that he was trying to make sense of Lewis's tragic death after the fact, and that he had the talent — apparently essential to American presidents — of distancing himself from problems he did not wish to reflect upon himself.

What is indisputable is that Meriwether Lewis was drinking prodigious quantities of alcohol in the last years of his life. Even the hints that percolate up through scattered documents are alarming.

In the last year of his life, from St. Louis, Lewis wrote about the problem of alcohol among the Indians. With his usual loftiness, he intoned, "I hold it an axiom incontravertible that it is more easy to introduce vice in all states of society than it is to eradicate it. . . ."[62] Indeed. He might have been writing of himself.

Of Courage Undaunted

Lewis had a reputation for courage and, in the minds of some, recklessness. Jefferson asked his cabinet members to suggest changes to his official instructions before sending them on to Lewis on June 20, 1803. Attorney General Levi Lincoln wrote, "From my ideas of Capt. Lewis he will be much more likely, in case of difficulty, to push too far, than to rec[e]de too soon. Would it not be well to change the term, '*certain* destruction' into *probable* destruction & to add — that these dangers are never to be encountered, which vigilance precaution & attention can secure against, at reasonable expense."[63] The President incorporated the Attorney General's suggestion. He wrote: "To your own discretion therefore must be left the degree of danger you may risk, and the point at which you should decline [conflict], only saying we wish you to err on the side of safety, and to bring back your party safe even if it be with less information."[64]

No one ever questioned Lewis's courage (this cannot be said of Jefferson). He had been known from childhood for possessing an intrepid character. The issue was whether at times he was too bold.

One of the few stories that emerged from Lewis's childhood is of his encounter with a raging bull. He was eight or nine years old, according to family legend. He was returning from a hunt with friends when an angry bull charged. Lewis calmly raised his rifle and shot the bull dead. This story may or may not exhibit rashness. It certainly exhibits undaunted courage. And Lewis's supreme confidence in himself so long as he held a rifle in his hands. Indeed, it is clear from the journals that Meriwether Lewis's sense of identity is intimately linked to his gun. "My gun reloaded," he wrote in Montana, "I felt confidence once more in my strength" [June 14, 1805].

More than twenty years later, at the Great Falls of the Missouri, Lewis nearly repeated the experience of his childhood. This time he was confronted not by one angry domestic bull, but three gigantic male bison. The bulls, "which wer feeding with a large herd about half a mile from me on my left, <singled> separated from the herd and ran full speed towards me." Lewis makes it clear that he might simply have withdrawn from the scene, but instead of running away he turned to meet the charging bison head on. "I thought at least to give them some amusement and altered my direction to meet them." As usual, his sense of humor is odd. As it turned out, no gunmanship was necessary this time. The bulls declined confrontation. " . . . when they arrived within a hundred yards they mad a halt, took a good view of me and retreated with precipitation," Lewis reports [June 14, 1805].

Later, summarizing a day that included tense encounters with a grizzly bear, a "tiger" of some sort, and the charging buffalo, Lewis admitted that the "curious adventures wore the impression on my mind of inchantment." Lewis was spooked. "It now seemed to me that all the beasts of the neighbourhood had made a league to distroy me, or that some fortune was disposed to amuse herself at my expence." In view of the disturbances of the day Lewis determined not to spend the night alone on the northern plains. "I then continued my rout homewards passed the buffaloe which I had killed, but did not think it prudent to remain all night at this place." Is it possible that part of the "inchantment" was a sense of *déjà vu*, a flash of consciousness from the cactus plains of Montana in early middle age, to the domestic pastures of Virginia and childhood? There are a number of indications that Meriwether Lewis was locked in an infantile stage: his orality, outbursts of anger, his inability to mate. . . . We cannot know what passed through his mind on June 14, 1805 alone on a landscape he felt he was the first civilized man to tread. We know only that he experienced "inchantment," that he had passed beyond the grid of rational, scientific, Enlightenment influence, and that he was not altogether comfortable in a zone of such great Medicine.

Lewis did not forget the magic of the Great Falls. A year later, on the return voyage, after a grizzly bear forced Hugh McNeal to spend much of a day in a tree, Lewis wrote, "there seems to be a sertain fatality attached to the neighbourhood of these falls, for there is always a chapter of accedents prepared for us during our residence at them" [July 15, 1806].

We know that Lewis had exhibited rashness as a young army officer. He had been court-martialed in November 1796, after a violent intrusion into a fellow officer's quarters, where he is alleged to have spoken in an ungentlemanly language, and challenged his adversary to a duel. Lewis was acquitted of the charges, but there is no indication that the basic facts were untrue. A moment's reflection would have convinced Lewis that nothing good could come of a quarrel with a fellow officer, but he was consumed — at that moment — by pride, anger, honor, and testosterone. It was a part of his character. Sometimes *daunted* courage is better.

There is not much evidence of rashness in the journals, however. It is true that Lewis was ready to fire on the Teton Sioux near what is now Pierre, South Dakota (September 1804), rather than provide them with even the token gift of tobacco they demanded by way of Missouri River passport, but his anger was understandable, and in some ways it was less pronounced than that of the characteristically more cheerful Clark. It is also true that when the feckless Charbonneau nearly sank the white pirogue in a squall on the Missouri in what is now western North Dakota, Lewis was tempted to swim the 300 yards between the shore and the crippled boat. He confesses:

> . . . finding I could not be heard, I for a moment forgot my own situation, and invollunarily, droped my gun, threw aside my shot pouch and was in the act of unbuttoning my coat, before I recollected the folly of the attempt I was about to make, which was to throw myself into the river and indevour to swim to the perogue; the perogue was three hundred yards distant the waves so high that a perogue could scarcely live in any situation, the water excessively could, and the stream rappid; had I undertaken this project therefore, there was a hundred to one but what I should have paid the forfit of my life for the madness of my project, but this had the perogue been lost, I should have valued but little— [May 14, 1805].

All that can be said of this is that William Clark, no less brave than his co-captain, would have been incapable of this response. Nor did Clark link his life's worth to the success of the Voyage of Discovery. Even so, Lewis did not swim to the stricken pirogue. His impulse may have been rash, but his behavior was prudent.

Beyond this the journals are free of any reports of what might be called rashness. In fact, Lewis is remarkably cool in crisis. A rash commander might well have let the Teton Sioux provoke bloodshed. In the skirmish with the Blackfeet on the upper Marias in July 1806, Lewis ordered his three companions not to take revenge on their adversaries, even though they virtually begged for permission to do so.

Usually cool in crisis, Lewis did engage in one rash act . . .

Lewis did, however, engage in one rash act among the Blackfeet. After the gunfight of July 27, 1806, on the south side of Two Medicine River, Lewis burned his antagonists' shields, bows and arrows, and other belongings. This makes sense. He was effectively eliminating their ability to strike back. He reclaimed the American flag he had bestowed on the party of Blackfeet. But he also left a ceremonial medal on one of the dead warriors " . . . that they might be informed who we were." Assuming this was one of the standard medals of the Expedition's provision list, it bore the image of President Jefferson on one face, and on the obverse face clasped hands, one Indian and one white, and the motto: "Peace and Friendship." This is irony indeed, and very dubious diplomacy. Lewis's pride is running before his good sense. From a purely economic point of view, it was a mistake to abandon the peace medal. It was, after all, one of the last tokens of value Lewis had in his inventory.

> *After Polyphemos has been blinded, he tries to get his fellow Cyclops to help him: "Good friends, Nobody is killing me by force or treachery." To which his friends answer, "If alone as you are None uses violence on you, why, there is no avoiding the sickness sent by great Zeus; so you had better pray to your father, the lord Poseidon."*[65]

In leaving the peace medal on the dead warrior's chest, Lewis committed an act of hubris worthy of Homer's epic hero Odysseus, who put out the lone eye of the Cyclops Polyphemos. When he first becomes the Cyclops' prisoner, Odysseus cleverly tells the monster that his name is No Body. This ruse protects Odysseus from retribution after he blinds the monster. (It also launches one of the lamest jokes of the ancient world.) But Odysseus is a hero, and his great heartedness will not permit him to remain anonymous in the wake of his victory over the one-eyed giant. He decides to taunt the monster from the relative safety of his retreating boat:

> 'Cyclops, if any mortal man ever asks you who it was
> that inflicted upon your eye this shameful blinding,
> tell him that you were blinded by Odysseus, sacker of cities.
> Laertes is his father, and he makes him home in Ithaka.'[66]

This moment of testosteronic heroism — worthy of swift-footed godlike Achilleus, but not the subtle "modern man" Odysseus — not only nearly costs Odysseus his life, but (far worse) delays his homecoming by years. At least Lewis did not provide the Blackfeet with his home address!

Meriwether Lewis had indulged his epic impulse on the far northern plains of Montana — and then got the hell out of there. He and his three companions rode 120 miles in twenty-four hours. Even before they made contact with the main party at the mouth of the Missouri and the Marias, Lewis reported " . . . that I could scarcely stand and the men complained of being in a similar situation" [July 28, 1806].

The Saint-Mémin painting of Lewis in ermine tippets became a part of the iconography of the Expedition. In this early print, featured on the cover of the first edition of Richard Dillon's biography and included in Charles Morrow Wilson's 1934 compendium of misinformation about Lewis entitled Meriwether Lewis of Lewis and Clark, *Lewis stands in one of the canoes in the shadow of Mount Hood as the seated Clark points out the way. Seated in the rear next to a soldier with plumed headgear behind Pomp in an elaborate cradle board and his mother, Sacagawea, is York, drawn with a huge (and, in the view of some, racist) grin. The work by an unknown artist began a tradition of Lewis and Clark hoisting the wrong flag: they carried one with fifteen stars and fifteen stripes, not thirteen and thirteen. Designer Wendell Minor reclothed Lewis in fringed buckskins and left the flag in a color version of the drawing above for David Lavender's 1988* The Way to the Western Sea: Lewis and Clark Across the Continent.

Musing the West

*I*n ***Walden***, Henry David Thoreau sought "to drive life into a corner and reduce it to its lowest terms," to determine, if possible, just what were the bare necessities of life. He called them life's "grossest groceries." Happiness and independence for Thoreau consisted of determining what humans cannot live without, and then finding the least onerous and most dignified way of obtaining those necessities. Thoreau was engaged in a bourgeois deprivation experiment. If a cabin at Walden Pond a mile or so from Ralph Waldo Emerson's Transcendentalist headquarters in Concord, Massachusetts, was a voluntary exercise in simplicity for Thoreau, the Voyage of Discovery was a kind of "forced march" towards "grossest groceries" for the members of the Lewis and Clark Expedition. Lewis, who died before Thoreau was born (July 12, 1817), was aware of this. In the course of his Expedition he pauses frequently to meditate on the supply of food, firepower, medicine, and Indian trade goods, and not merely from the perspective of a military commander anxious to keep enough calories in the stomachs of his troops. The enforced experiment in creative dining that was the Voyage of Discovery inspired Lewis on more than one occasion to ponder the philosophy of nutrition and the bare necessities of survival.

In fact, Meriwether Lewis was a philosopher in a way that William Clark was not (the contrast in the journals is striking) and in a way that even Thomas Jefferson was not. Jefferson was unendingly curious, but he was a common-sense materialist who did not lose much time on the imponderables of life. "When once we quit the basis of sensation," he wrote to John Adams in 1820, "all is in the wind. To talk of *immaterial* existences, is to talk of *nothings*. To say the human soul, angels, God, are immaterial, is to say, they are nothing or that there is no God, no angels, no soul." Once you know that Jefferson "lived temperately, eating little animal food, and that not as an aliment, so much as a condiment for the vegetables, which constitute my principal diet," you have his philosophy of nutrition.[67] Jefferson prided himself on being uncomplicated. Not so Meriwether Lewis.

Lewis has a propensity to wax philosophical. Among the Clatsops, noticing that old people are treated with respect chiefly because they contribute to the economic life of the tribe, he writes, "It appears to me that nature has been much more deficient in her filial tie than in any other of the strong affections of the human heart" [January 6, 1806]. This may be a misreading of lower Columbian culture, and it certainly carries with it some of Lewis's preconceptions about Indian habits, but it is admirable nevertheless. Meriwether Lewis is no mere explorer. He is playing Enlightenment scientist in the West. He is observing native peoples in something like a "state of nature." Because Indians are closer than the rest of us to their natural state (so the Enlightenment argument runs), it is easier to measure the nature of man among them than among civilized peoples whose nature has been distorted by social constructions. Lewis is out west examining what Shakespeare calls "unaccommodated man," man stripped of his pretensions, his clothes, and his institutions. What Lewis finds is not always admirable, but it is precisely the kind of inductive data that Jefferson and his fellow *philosophes* most sought.

For a Jeffersonian rationalist, Lewis at times seems surprisingly mystical. Noticing that the white pirogue seems particularly susceptible to accidents, Lewis writes, "it appears that the white perogue, which contains our most valuable stores, is attended by some evil gennii." A few days later he returns to this theme: "... I fear her evil gennii will play so many pranks with her that she will go to the bottomm some of those days—" [May 31, 1805]. When he encounters a grizzly bear, a "tiger," charging buffaloes, and a rattlesnake all in a single day at the Great Falls, Lewis — who is clearly unnerved by the experience — writes,

> I then continued my rout homewards passed the buffaloe which I had killed, but did not think it prudent to remain all night at this place which, really, from the succession of curious adventures wore the impression on my mind of inchantment; at sometimes for a moment I thought it might be a dream, but the prickley pears which pierced my feet very severely once in a while, particularly after it grew dark, convinced me that I was really awake, and that it was necessary to make the best of my way to camp.

Surely this would have been edited out, had Lewis lived, before the rationalist Mr. Jefferson was permitted to read an account of this adventure. Altogether alone in a far country, perhaps shaken by the realization of how utterly he depended on his gun for his safety and his identity, surrounded by animals that did not seem to yield to him primacy in the Great Chain of Being, feeling unmistakably vulnerable in a landscape that was by no means Edenic, Lewis candidly acknowledges psychological bewilderment. It is a monument to his soul that he was able to experience — and record — the dreamlike quality of pre-industrial Montana. In a sense, it proves that he *was* able to do justice to the sublimity of the Great Falls region after all. Interestingly, Lewis equates reality with pain. It is the spines of the prickly pear that prove to him that he is not dreaming, after all.

What an amazing moment this was. If he is not engaging in rhetoric, Meriwether Lewis is here admitting that in the heart of Montana, he was so enchanted that he could not be sure whether he was awake or asleep. Meriwether Lewis does not let down his guard very often. He is, after all, an army officer, a Virginia gentleman, the leader of a geopolitically important exploration party, and — not least — the protégé of Thomas Jefferson. But when he does, the result is always revealing and frequently remarkable. An emerging nation needs a pathfinder who is still capable of enchantment.

Every encounter is a potential mirror. Travel abroad enables the tourist not only to see his or her culture from a foreign perspective, to compare home habits with those of another society, but to ask of every cultural construct, every habit, every institution, "why it is so and not otherwise."[68] Sometimes travel awakens a sense of superiority — look how these silly natives do things when if they only thought about it they would . . . ? Sometimes it awakens a sense of inferiority — how come we are still doing things in so primitive a way when we might. . . ? Although Lewis seldom saw among native peoples a serious challenge to his own civilization's ways and means, he did not often fail to attend to the mirror of difference.

It was the age of Lemuel Gulliver. Jonathan Swift's great wanderer begins his travels sure that he represents the best of all possible worlds. Gulliver's cultural smugness is so great among the Lilliputians (miniature people) and the Brobdingnagians (giants) that he is either impervious to or flabbergasted by their implied or actual critiques of European civilization. Gulliver does not venture abroad as a critic of his home civilization. Nor does Meriwether Lewis. Gulliver's cultural arrogance is so great that it takes many challenges before his certitudes are shaken. So too, Lewis.

Even so, the mirrors accumulate in the course of the Swift's great narrative and even the complacent Gulliver is haunted by the king of the Brobdingnagians' response to Gulliver's exegesis of the institutions of western civilization. The king says:

> by what I have gathered from your own relation, and the answers I have with much pains wringed and extorted from you, I cannot but conclude the bulk of your natives to be the most pernicious race of little odious vermin that nature ever suffered to crawl upon the surface of the earth.

Jonathan Swift (1667-1745) is the greatest satirist in English literature. He focused his savage indignation on most of the habits and institutions of early modern Europe. He was a modest champion of the rights of the Irish. Gulliver's Travels *(1726) is one of the world's greatest —and nastiest — books. Jefferson admired it, and hoped that in America the Republican Gulliver would throw off the puny cords of the Federalist Lilliputians.*

Swift would be horrified to know that the world has refused to look into the fabulous mirror he erected, and that Gulliver's Travels *has for the most part been relegated (much bowdlerized) to the shelves of children's literature.*

Swift was, like Thomas Jefferson, an Enlightenment figure. The King of Brobdingnag speaks for Jefferson when he tells Gulliver, "that whoever could make two Ears of Corn, or two Blades of Grass to grow upon a spot of Ground where only one grew before, would deserve better of Mankind, and do more essential Service to his Country than the whole Race of Politicians put together."

And the pacific Jefferson agreed with Swift that "a Soldier *is a* Yahoo *hired to kill in cold Blood as many of his own Species, who have never offended him, as possibly he can."*

Gulliver's Travels *and the Journals of Lewis and Clark belong to the same genre. They are both travel notes from the Age of Exploration. To call one fiction and the other fact is to overlook their common focus on the challenge of the Other.*

Although Gulliver is not convinced by this savage attack on European culture, he cannot quite shake it off either. "Nothing but an extreme love of truth," he confesses, "could have hindered me from concealing this part of my story. . . . I was forced to rest with patience while my noble and most beloved country was so injuriously treated."

Gulliver's third voyage, to the utopian island of the Laputans, teaches him the limits of pure reason, western science, the quest for immortality, and the idea of progress. Interestingly enough, the zany universe of the Laputans, with its scientific projectors, virtuosos, geometrical cuts of meat, and hyper-rationalism is one that Thomas Jefferson might well have found compelling. There was more than a little of the bubble-headed projector in the Sage of Monticello. If ever a man believed that life might be brought to perfection by lists and grids, it was Thomas Jefferson. Only one President in American history made a chart of the seasonable availability of his 37 favorite vegetables at the greengrocers of Washington, D.C. It was Jefferson.

By the time Gulliver leaves the Houhyhynms after his fourth voyage, he has lost all his smugness. Indeed, in the face of a civilization of rational pastoral horses, Gulliver "goes native" and concludes that their civilization is not merely different from, but vastly superior to his own. With a mixture of shame and fascination, he now recognizes the dark side of his own civilization. Some cultural mirrors are better than others. When he observes the excremental Yahoos — primitive humans who behave no differently from the ravenous Shoshone in Lewis's experience — Gulliver finally sees a self-image that he can no longer ignore. The Yahoos are aggressive, rapacious, lustful, filthy, narcissistic, imbecilic, and nasty, and their national hug is unbearably repulsive. When a naked Yahoo girl embraces him, Gulliver writes, "I was never in my life so terribly frighted . . . she embraced me after a most fulsome manner; I roared as loud as I could. . . ." The shock of recognition undoes his soul. He is driven mad by what he sees of himself and his species in the projection of the bestial Yahoos.

Gulliver's re-entry, like that of Meriwether Lewis, was troubled. Having experienced what he experienced, and seen what he saw, he can no longer reconcile himself to Western Civilization, to England. Lewis upon return sleeps on the floor on animal skins. Gulliver sleeps with the horses in the barn. "I began last week," he writes, "to permit my wife to sit at dinner with me, at the farthest end of a long table, and to answer (but with the utmost brevity) the few questions I ask her. Yet the smell of a Yahoo continuing very offensive, I always keep my nose well stopped with rue, lavender, or tobacco leaves. And although it be hard for a man late in life to remove old habits, I am not altogether out of hopes in some time to suffer a neighbour Yahoo in my company, without the apprehensions I am yet under of his teeth or his claws." Gulliver overcame his mania with rue and lavender, Lewis with grain alcohol. Gulliver was more fortunate than Meriwether Lewis; he had taken a wife before his travels disturbed his peace of mind. Imagine poor Gulliver courting the ladies after his return from the final voyage.

It can be argued, I think, that Gulliver's conversion experience is only partly owing to what he considers the cultural superiority of those rational horses the Houhyhnhnms. He has, by now, been worn down by a long period of travel. There is perhaps an accumulative effect of seeing life differently organized again and again and again by cultures that seem to manage quite well according to standards wildly different from those of eighteenth-century Europe. It may be that at some point Gulliver would have lost his sense of confidence, his cultural identity, no matter what sort of beings he met on the road. He was gone too long. He looked into too many mirrors. Too much time at the raw end of the chain of being can unfit one for the artificialities of civilization. In Lewis's case there were hints all along. His satiric comment on the desirability of "insippid food" prairie artichokes (see above, page 13) and his comparison of his meal of buffalo and beans to the dainties of "our epicures" back in civilization (page 19) are hints that Lewis could not help but pierce through the thin veneer of the civilization that shaped him, and for which he longed with such eagerness from Fort Clatsop. His endless musings about food are an exploration of the *sine qua non* that holds body and soul together.

No single mirror breaks Gulliver's confidence. It is apparently the accumulation of challenges — of glimpses into difference, of reminders of the arbitrariness of his own tradition, of intimations of the flimsiness of human values — that dismantle Gulliver. The fate of Meriwether Lewis was virtually identical.

It is not merely a coincidence that Jonathan Swift wrote *Gulliver's Travels* in the age of exploration. Gulliver, like Meriwether Lewis, is an explorer/adventurer who takes himself too seriously. Surely it is the case that no greater mirror has ever been thrown up to the pretensions of European civilization than the discovery of the New World.

Lewis's propensity to explore the human condition, and his own identity, by way of the peoples he met is especially pronounced among the Shoshone. They are his Yahoos. Somehow the Shoshones proved to be the critical cultural mirror. There are several reasons for this. First, Lewis was comparatively alone among the Shoshone. Most of the party, and most particularly William Clark, were manhandling the boats among the upper reaches of the Missouri's feeder streams during this crucial period. Lewis is not at his best when he meets Indians alone — among the Blackfeet the result will be disastrous. Second, the fate of the Expedition appeared to depend on a successful encounter with the Shoshone Indians, and preliminary indications had not been particularly favorable. Third, Meriwether Lewis was about to celebrate his thirty-first birthday and his mood was not particularly upbeat. Finally, and most important, by now many of the markers of European civilization had been peeled away from Meriwether Lewis and his troops.

The whiskey was gone. Most of the cloth clothing had long since disintegrated. Some of the company — presumably both captains— appear to have been shaving regularly, but everyone was sunburned, especially now that William Clark's umbrella had been lost in the flash flood at the Great Falls. Order has yielded to dishevelry. By now they were a tatterdemalion crew.

The tether to civilization had been stretched to the breaking point.

Lewis made contact with the Shoshone Indians on August 13, 1805. Clark caught up on August 17, 1805. That four-day period may be the most important of the entire Expedition. It is certainly critical as a window on the soul of Meriwether Lewis. The challenges Lewis faced were gigantic. First, he had to convince the Shoshone, to whom he was a stranger and possibly an enemy, that he was in fact a friend and a harbinger of good things to come. He had to do this, of course, without an adequate language interpreter. Then he had to convince the Shoshone to venture out of their zone of security in the Bitterroot Mountains down onto the plains near the source of the Missouri River. This was asking them to risk an encounter with their enemies — the Pahkees — merely because some assertive stranger requested it — with no serious talk of recompense, and certainly no guarantee of safety. Perhaps most unnerving to Meriwether Lewis, he had to convince the Shoshone that he was not an Indian! " . . . my over shirt being of the Indian form my hair deshivled and skin well browned with the sun I wanted no further addition to make me a complete Indian in appearance. . ." [August 16, 1805]. Lewis found himself in the anomalous position of having to prove that he was a white man among a people who had never seen a white man before. He rolled up his sleeve to reveal the comparatively pale skin of his inner arm. He shouted "*tab-ba-bone*" [August 11, 1805], which he had convinced himself meant "white man," but which almost certainly meant "stranger" or possibly even "enemy." Lewis should have realized that a culture that has never seen a white man cannot be expected to have a precise name for one.

When Lewis finally makes contact with an elderly woman and a teenaged girl, he attempts to reassure them by painting their faces with vermilion. Presumably he has been taught this trick by Sacagawea and not merely concocted a pan-Indian "encounters" ritual from white man's lore. Among Indians, Lewis is apparently incapable of straightforward description. He writes, "I now painted their tawny cheeks with some vermillion which with this nation is emblematic of peace" [August 13, 1805]. Why tawny? This adjective belittles the terrified Shoshone individuals upon whom the fate of the Expedition might well rest. Lewis employs the adjective "tawny" to distance himself from the Indians. He is sunburned; they are tawny.

Sixty warriors gallop into the picture, ready to fight. With his characteristic undaunted courage, Lewis advances alone, deliberately leaving his gun behind, until he is fifty paces ahead of his tiny party. Suddenly all is joy and hospitality. Disarmed by the sight of trinkets and by the gushing testimony of the three women who first encountered Lewis, the Shoshone greet the strangers with effusive affection. A vulnerable, potentially fatal situation has turned to sweet harmony. The Captain of the Corps of Discovery has reason to be enormously grateful, immensely relieved. Instead, he unleashes a burst of cultural arrogance: "these men then advanced and embraced me very affectionately in their way which is by puting their left arm over you wright sholder clasping your back, while they apply their left cheek to yours and frequently vociforate the word *âh-hi'-e, âh-hi'-e* that is, I am much pleased, I am much rejoiced. bothe parties now advanced and we wer all carresed and besmeared with their grease and paint till I was heartily tired of the national hug" [August 13, 1805]. What could be more remarkable than the picture of the self-important, stiff, fragile Meriwether Lewis in an unwilling, full-bodied embrace with naked men who do not respect European spatial boundaries? It is the stuff of comedy, were it not for the genocidal madness of the century that Meriwether Lewis helped to open in the West.

The words, "affectionately in their way," "vociforate," "besmeared," and of course, "I was heartily tired of the national hug," reveal condescension and arrogance, but they pale beside Lewis's lecture to the Shoshone leader Cameahwait two days later when the chief reveals that his fellow tribesmen fear that Lewis is planning to lead them into an ambush. Lewis gathers up all of his ethnocentrism to declare:

> I told Cameahwait that I was sorry to find that they had put so little confidence in us, that I knew they were not acquainted with whitemen and therefore could forgive them. that among whitemen it was considered disgracefull to lye or entrap an enimy by falsehood. I told him if they continued to think thus meanly of us that they might rely on it that no whitemen would ever come to trade with them or bring them arms and amunition and that if the bulk of his nation still entertained this opinion I still hoped that there were some among them that were not affraid to die. . . [August 16, 1805].

There is something appalling in this, not just because Lewis attempts to manipulate the justly-apprehensive Cameahwait the way a bad parent coerces a child, but for the outrageous fraud of declaring that "whitemen" never lie to or entrap an enemy. Perhaps Lewis has in mind the French betrayal of the black rebel leader Toussaint L'Overture in St. Domingo in 1802, accomplished with the blessing of the Jefferson administration.

"White men never lie," says Meriwether Lewis, and then he immediately lies: unless Cameahwait cooperates, "no whitemen would ever come to trade with them." Lewis's claim — that white men never tell a lie — is wildly erroneous in the face of American history even up to August 1805, and of course merely obscene in the face of white-Indian relations of the later nineteenth century. But Mr. Jefferson's protégé is far from finished. Lewis shames Cameahwait into redoubling his efforts to secure a Shoshone escort for the American party, and then Lewis gloats over the success of his manipulation:

> I soon found that I had touched him on the right string; to doubt the bravery of a savage is at once to put him on his metal. he now mounted his horse and haranged his village a third time; the perport of which as he afterwards told me was to inform them that he would go with us. . . [August 15, 1805] .

Lewis hustles Cameahwait and his warriors along "while I had them in the humour," and then pauses to engage in a little sociology:

> this may serve in some measure to illustrate the capricious disposition of those people, who never act but from the impulse of the moment. they were now very cheerfull and gay, and two hours ago they looked as sirly as so many imps of satturn [August 15, 1805].

To complete his portrait of the Shoshone, Lewis describes in lurid detail the way the tribe — a refugee culture, victims of an arms war touched off by Hudson Bay traders — devours a deer that Drewyer managed to kill. Lewis writes, " . . . when they arrived where the deer was . . . they dismounted and ran in tumbling over each other like a parcel of famished dogs each seizing and tearing away a part of the intestens which had been previously thrown out by Drewyer who killed it" [August 16, 1805]. They were, in short, something less than human. They behaved like a "parcel of famished dogs," not men. "I really did not untill now think that human nature ever presented itself in a shape so nearly allyed to the brute creation." The Shoshone eat gross groceries indeed. Had Lewis been as well-educated as his patron, he might have flashed from Shoshone Cove to King Lear evaluating the beggar Poor Tom on the blasted heath: "Is man no more than this? . . . Thou art the thing itself; unaccommodated man is no more but such a poor, bare, forked animal as thou art."[69] Lewis declares that "I viewed these poor starved divils with pity and compassion." No doubt he is telling the truth, but to the reader of the early twenty-first century it feels more like contempt and, at times, ridicule. Clark could not have written such prose. He could neither have equaled Lewis in literary flair nor sunk to such sarcasm and condescension.

Without Sacagawea, Lewis had somehow made contact with the Shoshone chief Cameahwait and managed to alleviate at least some of his apprehensions. Drewyer's prowess as a hunter helped. Somehow Lewis had cajoled and browbeaten the chief into agreeing to accompany him to the rendezvous point with Clark. Somehow he had managed to keep Cameahwait and a portion of his warriors on task in spite of growing fears that Lewis was leading them into an ambush. With so much at stake, Lewis did not rest well. "I slept but little," he wrote on August 16, "as might be well expected, my mind dwelling on the state of the expedition which I have ever held in equal estimation with my own existence, and the fait of which appeared at this moment to depend in a great measure upon the caprice of a few savages who are ever as fickle as the wind." The stresses were stupendous, and Lewis — as usual in such circumstances — imagined the collapse of the Expedition. It is as difficult for us to imagine the fragility of this encounter as it is to believe William Clark could have responded to these circumstances in this way.

This is one of the most significant moments in American history. Lewis, a civilized man alone in a landscape where no civilized man has gone before, reduced in appearance to Indianness, desperately trying to hold his mission together, finds it harder and harder to maintain his sense of himself. He is, in short, having an identity crisis in Montana.

When Lewis, Cameahwait, and the warrior rump of the Shoshone finally approach the rendezvous point on August 16, Lewis finally turned into an Indian.

> we now dismounted and the Chief with much cerimony put tippets about our necks such as they temselves woar I redily perceived that this was to disguise us and owed it's origine to the same cause already mentioned. to give them further confidence I put my cocked hat with feather on the chief and my over shirt being of the Indian form my hair dishivled and skin well browned with the sun I wanted no further addition to make me a complete Indian. . . .

"To make me a complete Indian." This cannot have been very satisfying for a man so adamant about cultural hierarchies. And of course it leads to the kind of question the Enlightenment liked to ask in theory but perhaps not always in fact. What is the difference — on a hot August day in 1805 in western Montana, approximately 3000 river miles from the White House, in the heart of American darkness — between the Anglo and the Shoshone, between Meriwether Lewis and a chief named Cameahwait, between the civilized and the savage man? The answer appears to be contempt.

Lewis's next sentence is even more revealing: "the men followed my example [in changing clothes with the Indians] and we were soon completely metamorphosed." In searching for lan-

Ovid (43 BCE-17 CE), was the most popular of all Roman poets. Although his works are witty, erotic, and often parodic, he somehow managed to survive the Christian interregnum in European history. The theme of Metamorphoses *is magical transformation: gods into animals; maidens into trees, flowers, and quadrupeds. Among other things, the* Metamorphoses *is the best ancient compendium of Greek and Roman mythology.*

guage to explain this extraordinary and unprecedented moment, Lewis finds his way to the Roman mythographer Ovid. He could not have chosen a finer word than "metamorphosed" if he had taken months to revise his journals. The white man has become the Indian and the Indian the white man. This is one of those instances when every reader of the journals of Lewis and Clark must rejoice that Lewis did not live to produce his three-volume narrative of the Voyage of Discovery, to replace his first impressions with studied prose. In his field journal Lewis opened a series of marvelous windows on his soul. It was a strange and often troubled soul. And though what he writes on these occasions does not always do him credit as a Jeffersonian, it usually helps to excavate the terrain of his consciousness. One cannot write that many words under extreme conditions and not reveal a great deal about one's values, assumptions, prejudices, doubts, aspirations — and bowels.

Alone among naked men, Meriwether Lewis keeps asking himself Shakespearean questions. What is a man? What is the difference between Prospero and Caliban? If you look like an Indian, and dress like an Indian, and eat like an Indian, sleep like an Indian, and wander like an Indian in Indian country, how can you be said to be different from an Indian? How do you maintain your identity as a civilized man when all the accoutrements of your life have become savage? "What is a man," asks Hamlet, "if his chief good and market of his time be but to sleep and feed? A beast, no more?"[70] How do you convince a savage that you are not a

Shakespeare's last play The Tempest (1611) was influenced by the discovery of the New World. The Renaissance prince Prospero and his daughter Miranda are shipwrecked on a mysterious island that in some respects feels like America. Caliban, "a born devil, on whose nature nurture can never stick," is Shakespeare's dark portrait of an Indian. The name Caliban is probably a play on cannibal. Caliban is indeed brutish, but Shakespeare makes him capable, too, of generosity of spirit and a pre-alphabetic lyricism that comes from his rootedness in nature. He is at times a Noble Savage. At the end of the play Prospero is able to look into the mirror of Caliban and see a primitive —but recognizable — cousin to himself.

savage? Such questions drove King Lear insane. But in spite of the fact that Lewis has come to eat dog and the intestines of quadrupeds, defecate in the woods, wear animal skins, sleep under the stars, and speak in sign language, he is never able, like Shakespeare's Prospero, to turn to Cameahwait/Caliban and say, "This thing of darkness I acknowledge mine."[71] It turns out that Lewis cannot embrace the central truths of life any more than he can embrace a naked Shoshone. Lewis did not embrace the shadow. Instead he projected it onto the "vilest miscreants of the savage race" (see page 60), including poor Cameahwait, who strained so continuously to trust the contemptuous stranger. And he drowned it in alcohol.

The paradox of Meriwether Lewis is that he had the genius to look into the mirror again and again in the West, but never to reach a Shakespearean insight — or resignation — about the commonality of the human condition. He continued to see himself as the acme of the Enlightenment even after he had "metamorphosed" into what he condemned as savagery. He could never embrace the national hug. Clark, meanwhile, was able to come to terms with almost anything so long as he need not relish the flesh of the dog. The difference between Meriwether Lewis and William Clark is that Clark looked into the heart of things and shrugged, Lewis shuddered. In essence, Clark is a life-affirming comic figure, Lewis a tragic hero. Clark like Odysseus lived a full productive life. Lewis like Achilleus died in his prime.

If you wish to understand what happened "out there" to Meriwether Lewis you must meditate his encounter with the Shoshone like a koan.

In the end Lewis has only one last marker of civilization — his gun. That is all that distinguishes

The paradox of Meriwether Lewis is that he had the genius to look into the mirror again and again in the West, but never to reach a Shakespearean insight — or resignation — about the commonality of the human condition.

him from a people who approach — in his mind — the "brute creation." Lewis and Clark were willing to trade almost anything — agricultural implements, sewing tools, clothing, whiskey, even sex — to obtain what they needed or wanted, but up until now they had clung to their guns with heroic resolve. Among the Shoshone Lewis is in extremis. He is so desperate to succeed with Cameahwait that he relinquishes even his gun. Now he is entirely vulnerable. Suddenly Meriwether Lewis has nothing left to lose.

> when we arrived in sight at the distance of about 2 miles I discovered to my mortification that the party had not arrived, and the Indians slackened their pace. I now scarcely new what to do and feared every moment when they would halt altogether, I now determined to restore their confidence cost what it might and therefore gave the Chief my gun and told him that if his enimies were in those bushes before him that he could defend himself with that gun, that for my own part I was not affraid to die and if I deceived him he might make what uce of the gun he thought proper or in other words that he might shoot me [August 16, 1805].

Lewis succeeded in keeping Cameahwait on task, but the cost was staggering. The "sublime dandy" who obsessed over the trim on an officer's coat has become a gunless man in skins who subsists on the entrails of quadrupeds and communicates by gesticulation.

Among the Indians

When Meriwether Lewis called Indians "Children!" in his diplomatic speeches, he meant it. On the whole he saw Indians as capricious, unreliable, immature and potentially treacherous. He saw them as creatures to be coddled or bullied, beings who could be manipulated to further American ends. Perhaps he was willing to pursue Mr. Jefferson's Enlightenment agenda as far as it was practicable in the West, but just beneath the surface of official policy, beneath the patina of the Noble Savage mythology Jefferson imposed on him on the home court of the White House, Lewis had deep permanent misgivings about Indians. These misgivings grew with time. If the West stripped Lewis of the trappings of civilization, it also stripped him of whatever positive notions he held about Indians.

It is true that even the Indian-loving Jefferson — who collected vocabularies and artifacts, who studied Indian political systems, who envied Indian "democracy" and individualism, who swooned over Indian oratory, who held up Indians as living refutations of the European degeneracy theory of Buffon — even Jefferson spoke to Indian delegations with a kind of "Indian baby talk" that seems astonishingly condescending to the modern ear. To the Mandan Nation Jefferson wrote, "We are descended from the old nations which live beyond the great water, but we and our forefathers have been so long here that we seem like you to have grown out of this land."[72] To a delegation partly made up of Lewis and Clark-sponsored chiefs, Jefferson said on January 6, 1806, "We are become as numerous as the leaves of the trees, and tho' we do not boast, we do not fear any nation. . . . My children, we are strong, we are numerous as the stars in the heavens, and we are all gun-men."[73] Hamilton would have snorted at Jefferson's claims to be a "gun-man." Jefferson loved Indians, but he never once permitted his romance to get in the way of his political agenda, which was to dispossess Native Americans of their territories as peacefully as possible, and as ruthlessly as necessary.

The best that can be said is this. Meriwether Lewis left the White House bearing a fair portion of Thomas Jefferson's optimism, curiosity, and benevolence. He was surely buoyed by Jeffersonian principles, even if he had secret misgivings about Mr. Jefferson's more optimistic notions about nature, climate, the pastoral dream, and American Indians. He may have felt that the President was naïve, but he could not have avoided being inspired by the President's idealistic sense of purpose. In spite of the nearly-disastrous encounter with the Teton Sioux, Lewis managed to carry something of Jefferson's magnanimity almost to the Pacific Ocean. The benign encounters with the Mandan, the Flatheads, and the Nez Percé may even have reinforced the Jeffersonian notion that an Indian was a republican in a loincloth.

It is also clear that whatever his private attitudes, Lewis brought a strong sense of responsibility and honor to his relations with Indians. On two of the three occasions when he felt he had cheated or mistreated Indians, he expresses uneasiness. Among the Shoshone, when Lewis lied to his host Cameahwait and pretended that the note he had himself left for Clark on a tree was in fact a note from Clark announcing *his* imminent arrival, Lewis confesses, " . . . I now had recource to a stratagem in which I thought myself justifyed by the occasion, but which I must confess set a little awkard" [August 16,1805]. Pressed by sheer necessity, Lewis and Clark set themselves up as country doctors on their return journey through the Columbia basin in 1806. Lewis acknowledges that they are essentially offering placebo medicines. "this occurrence added to the benefit which many of them experienced from the eyewater we gave them about the same time has given them an exalted opinion of our medicine. my friend Capt. C. is their favorite phisician and has already received many applications. in our present situation I think it pardonable to continue this desception for they will not give us any provision without compensation in merchandize and our stock is now reduced to a mere handfull. We take care to give them no article which can possibly oinjure them" [May 5, 1806]. Here Lewis admits that the Expedition is driven by necessity, and he takes refuge in a version of the Hippocratic Oath, but he does not pretend that he is proud of his placebo distribution operation.

Only once does Lewis breach his code of encounter ethics without any expression of remorse. In mid-March 1806, unable to purchase a much-needed canoe from Chief Coboway on the Pacific coast, the Expedition finally just appropriates it. On this occasion Lewis merely provides a tantalizing rationalization: "we yet want another canoe, and as the Clatsops will not sell us one at a price which we can afford to give we will take one from them in lue of the six Elk which they stole from us in the winter— [March 17, 1806].

Somehow the pool of good will was gone shortly into the return voyage in 1806. A few geographical imperatives (and side trips) aside, by now the members of the Lewis and Clark Expedition just wanted to go home, as quickly and as painlessly as possible. The purposefulness, the uncertainty, and the sense of wonder of the outbound journey were gone now. There was nothing much left to discover. By the time the Expedition began its long bankrupt return journey, Lewis's attitude towards Indians was simple: give us what we request on demand, without balking at the price we are willing to pay; make no demands on us; unless we need you, stay out of our way.

When several members of the Wahclellah tribe stole Lewis's beloved dog Seaman, Lewis sent three of his men in pursuit. His orders? " . . . if they made the least resistance or difficulty in surrendering the dog to fire on them" [April 11, 1806]. The Wahclellahs wisely relinquished Seaman when they saw the menacing faces of Lewis's posse. On the same day the exasperated captain wrote, "we ordered the centinel to keep them out of camp, and informed them by signs that if they made any further attempts to steal our property or insulted our men we should put them to instant death." The chief of the tribe informed Lewis that the trouble was the work of " . . . two very bad men among the Wah-clel-lahs who had been the principal actors in these scenes of outradge. . . ." Lewis is skeptical. He has heard this sort of excuse before. Ten days later, when an Indian pilfered an iron socket from a canoe pole, Lewis erupts in violence. "I . . . gave him several severe blows and mad the men kick him out of camp." It had been a hard day. First a stolen tomahawk, now the socket. "I now informed the indians that I would shoot the first of them that attempted to steal an article from us. that we were not affraid to fight them, that I had it in my power at that moment to kill them all and set fire to their houses. . . ." Then he partly recovers his composure: "... but it was not my wish to treat them with severity provided they would let my property alone. that I would take their horses if I could find out the persons who had stolen the tommahawks, but that I had reather loose the property altogether than take the hose of an inosent person" [April 21, 1806]. Captain Lewis has hurtled from pettiness to nobility in a single sentence. It is clear that Lewis is struggling to behave like a Jeffersonian in the far West, when all his impulses are, in fact, Jacksonian. So far as can be determined, Lewis's "several severe blows" were the first gesture of violence by a member of the Expedition toward a Native American.

One day later the Indians stole a saddle blanket. "I sent the Indian woman [Sacagawea] on," he wrote, "to request Capt. C. to halt the party and send back some of the men to my assistance being determined either to make the indians deliver the robe or birn their houses. they have vexed me in such a manner by such repeated acts of villany that I am quite disposed to treat them with every severyty . . ." [April 22, 1806]. Again, he struggles to regain control: "their defenseless state pleads forgivness so far as rispects their lives."

Lewis and Clark were so vexed by the pilfering, the capricousness, the higgling, the lying promises, and the "Indian giving" of the Columbia Indians on the return journey that they broke up their canoes — when they ceased to need them — rather than sell them at firesale rates. Lewis reports, "I ordered all the spare poles, paddles and the ballance of our canoe put on the fire as the morning was cold and also that not a particle should be left for the benefit of the indians" [April 21, 1806].

And there is, of course, the notorious puppy incident of May 5, 1806. A Nez Percé boy made the grave mistake of taunting Captain Meriwether Lewis about the barbarism of his diet. Worse, he turned the concepts of savage and civilized man upside down:

> while at dinner, an indian fellow verry impertinently threw a poor half starved puppy nearly into my plait by way of derision for our eating dogs and laughed very heartily at his own impertinence; I was so provoked at his insolence that I caught the puppy and threw it with great violence at him and struk him on the breast and face, siezed my tomahawk and shewed him by signs if he repeated his insolence I would tommahawk him, the fellow withdrew apparently much mortifyed and I continued my repast *on dog* without any further molestation.

One source of Lewis's rage, surely, is the fact that the normal cultural hierarchies have been reversed. Far from the tables of "our epicures," Meriwether has momentarily lost his cultural superiority. Suddenly he is the savage and a Nez Percé "fellow" is the arbiter of culinary taste. Lewis's rage is still high at the time of his writing. Notice the angry repetitions of key words: "impertinent," "insolence," "tomahawk," "fellow."

When he met an Indian who behaved honorably, Lewis was astonished. Black Cat of the upper Mandan village won his respect.

On February 8, 1805, Lewis wrote, "this man possesses more integrety, firmness, intelligence and perspicucty of mind than any indian I have met with in this quarter." So far so good. Then Lewis finishes his sentence: "and I think with a little management he may be made a usefull agent in furthering the views of our government." Perhaps he thought Black Cat was partly Welsh.

Lewis's patience with Indians seems to have run out sooner than William Clark's. One key difference between the captains can be seen in their responses to Indians generally. Clark seems to have been an open-minded pragmatist with respect to the Indians they encountered. Perhaps because he was dutifully attempting to carry Jeffersonian optimism and the romance of the Noble Savage into the wilderness, Lewis seems to have been more disappointed by Indians than was Clark, who almost always found it possible to take Indians for what they were. One scours Clark's journal entries in vain for signs of exasperation.

The difference in attitude between Lewis and Clark can be seen in their responses to Sacagawea. On July 28, 1805, Sacagawea found herself "precisely on the spot" from which she had been abducted by Hidatsa raiders in her childhood. Lewis writes, "*Sah-cah-gar-we-a* or Indian woman was one of the female prisoners taken at that time; tho' I cannot discover that she shews any immotion of sorrow in recollecting this event, or of joy in being again restored to her native country; if she has enough to eat and a few trinkets to wear I believe she would be perfectly content anywhere.—" Not only is Lewis wrong, but he is essentially denying Sacagawea human status. He sees her not as stoic, but robotic. It may be that Sacagawea had long since determined that she could not make any connection with Meriwether Lewis, and therefore played the stoic in his presence more than when she was in the company of William Clark. Or it may be that Lewis simply could not penetrate what he took to be her savagery. He could see an Indian woman's bubbies, but not her heart. It is undeniable that

Lewis felt more sympathy for birds, for his dog Seaman, for a dying buffalo, even for Charbonneau, than for Sacagawea.

Where we stand depends on where we sit. On August 17, 1805, Clark sees something quite different in Sacagawea. When she first saw her people again after at least five years of separation, Clark reports that "The Intertrepeter [Charbonneau] & Squar . . . danced for the joyful Sight. . . ." It is quite clear that Clark warmed up to Sacagawea more than did Meriwether Lewis. To Clark, not Lewis, she gave twelve dozen weasels' tail for Christmas 1805 at Fort Clatsop. It is Clark, not Lewis, who "checked [i.e. rebuked] our interpreter for Strikeing his woman at their Dinner" on August 14, 1805. It seems clear that Clark served as Sacagawea's protector on the Voyage of Discovery. The lone woman on an eighteen month journey with more than thirty virile young men would need a patron — and Charbonneau may not have had enough of the right stuff to serve in that capacity. It is Clark, not Lewis, who offered to bring the Charbonneau family to St. Louis after the Expedition. It is characteristically with Clark, not Lewis, that the Charbonneau family travels whenever the Corps of Discovery splits up on the journey. Just three days after the Charbonneau family withdrew from the Expedition and began to settle again into life at the Mandan and Hidatsa villages, William Clark wrote one of the most remarkable letters of his life. On August 20, 1806, at the bottom of what is now North Dakota, Clark wrote to Charbonneau repeating his offer to bring the whole family to St. Louis to live under his patronage and supervision. "Your woman who accompanied you that long dangerous and fatigueing rout to the Pacific Ocean and back diserved a greater reward for her attention and services on that rout than we had in our power to give her at the Mandans."[74] It is hard to know quite what to make of this letter, but this much is certain: Meriwether Lewis could not have written it.

Among the Shoshone, Lewis feels confidence that the canoes which his men sank in a pond for safe keeping during their trans-Bitterroot journey will be safe, but not because he trusts the

Shoshone: "the Indians have promised to do them no intentional injury and believe they are too lazy at any rate to give themselves the trouble to raise them from their present situation in order to cut or birn them" [August 23, 1805].

Lewis's attitude towards Indians is unendingly condescending. On those occasions when he finds himself praising Indians, he always expresses surprise. Thus, after admiring the conical rain hats of the Clatsops, and ordering custom hats for himself and William Clark, and then finding those hats so efficient at keeping out rain that he ordered hats for everyone in the company, Lewis writes that the canoes, along with "the woodwork and sculpture of these people as well as these hats and their waterproof baskets evince an ingenuity by no means common among the Aborigenes of America" [February 22, 1806].

Lewis's misgiving about Indians are never far from the surface. Even though his experiences with Indians were, on the whole, remarkably satisfying and peaceful, even though the lower Columbia Indians had shown considerable hospitality to the Corps of Discovery, Lewis on February 20, 1806 gives vent to a racist fantasy far below the surface of Thomas Jefferson's benevolence:

> . . . notwithstanding their apparent friendly disposition, their great averice and hope of plunder might induce them to be treacherous. at all events we determined allways to be on our guard as much as the nature of our situation will permit us, and never place ourselves at the mercy of any savages. we well know, that the treacher of the aborigenes of America and the too great confidence of our countrymen in their sincerity and friendship, has caused the distruction of many hundreds of us. so long have our men been accustomed to a friendly intercourse with the natives, that we find it difficult to impress on their minds the necessity of always being on their guard with rispect to them. this confidence on our part, we know to be the effect of a series of uninterrupted friendly intercouse, but the well known treachery of the natives by no means entitle them to such confidence, and we must check it's growth in our own minds, as well as those of our men, by recollecting ourselves, and repeating to our men, that our preservation depends on

> never loosing sight of this trait in their character, and being always prepared to meet it in whatever shape it may present itself.—

This is the sort of prose one would expect from George Armstrong Custer, not Meriwether Lewis. This from a man who (unlike Clark) had never fought an Indian during his years in the trans-Allegheny West. It is not clear what demons swam in the soul of Meriwether Lewis, but it is certain that his sense of the enormous superiority of his own civilization, the lore-and-experience he had gathered from his time on the Virginia, the Georgia, and later the Ohio frontiers, and the disappointment of whatever Jeffersonian notions he carried with him into the West, reduced Lewis to the twin poles of Eurocentrism and racism, particularly on the homeward journey in 1806.

It is not clear what demons swam in the soul of Meriwether Lewis, but it is certain that his sense of the enormous superiority of his own civilization . . . reduced Lewis to the twin poles of Eurocentrism and racism. . . .

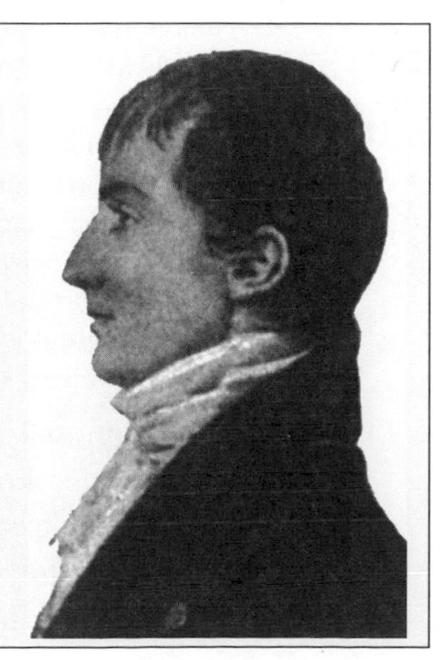

This drawing of Meriwether Lewis by an unknown artist, featured in many early editions of World Book Encyclopedia, *bears a striking resemblance to images of Bonaparte, especially the hair style. Lewis's classmate Peachy Gilmer said, "His person was stiff and without grace; bowlegged, awkward, formal and almost without flexibility. It bore to my vision a very strong resemblance to Buonaparte."*[75]

The dark despair that round him blew[76]

There is something sweetly melancholy in Lewis's journal entry for January 1, 1806 from Fort Clatsop:

> This morning I was awoke at an early hour by the discharge of a volley of small arms, which were fired by our party in front of our quarters to usher in the new year; this was the only mark of rispect which we had it in our power to pay this celebrated day. our repast of this day tho' better than that of Christmass, consisted principally in the anticipation of the 1st day of January 1807, when in the bosom of our friends we hope to participate in the mirth and hilarity of the day, and when with the zest given by recollection of the present, we shall completely, both mentally and corporally, enjoy the repast which the hand of civilization has prepared for us. at present we were content with eating our boiled Elk and wappetoe, and solacing our thirst with our only beverage *pure water*. two of our hunters who set out this morning reterned in the evening having killed two bucks elk; they presented Capt. Clark and myself each a marrow-bone and tonge, <each> on which we suped.

The word "homesick" was coined in 1798, just in time for this moment. Meriwether Lewis is undeniably homesick, though he does not use the neologism. He also appears to be ready for a drink. The home he longs for might well be the President's house in Washington, D.C. During his two winters with President Jefferson, Lewis enjoyed a "repast which the hand of civilization" [i.e. Jefferson's White House staff — largely black] . . . prepared for him. Jefferson held two White House receptions each year: one on the nation's birthday, July 4, and one on New Year's Day. Lewis apparently expects to spend New Year's Day 1807 with his patron — "with the zest given by recollection of the present." And he did. We know he was on hand to present the Mandan leader Sheheke to the President in the White House on December 30, 1806 and that he attended the President's New Year's reception two days later, as did the Mandan Indian delegation. The fare, no doubt, was quintessentially Jeffersonian. One wonders what Sheheke thought of Mr. Jefferson's Bordeaux? Notice that Lewis — from Fort Clatsop — is anticipating both physical and mental satisfactions of next year. William Clark was an interesting man, but he was no Thomas Jefferson. How Lewis, a man with pretensions to learning and civility, must have longed for the moment when he would brief the philosopher President on the wonders of his Expedition.

The new orthodoxy is that Meriwether Lewis was a manic depressive, a man afflicted with bipolar personality disorder. This is probably true — considerable evidence points in this direction — but it is always dangerous to impose twenty-first-century concepts on an eighteenth-century man. In writing about the past it is always essential to be aware that we live on this side of the continental divide of Sigmund Freud (1856-1939). It seems certain that the men and women of Jefferson's world would not only find themselves unrecognizable in the amateur psychoanalytical portraits we draw of them, but would reject out of hand such intrusions into the *sancta sanctorum* of their souls.

The fact that Meriwether Lewis almost certainly committed suicide in 1809 has inspired students of the Expedition to cast a net of despair over his whole life and achievement. Lewis was frequently and (in some regards) unaccountably silent during his time in the West. This, we are routinely informed, is because he was too depressed to write. Is this true? Possibly — but there may be other reasonable explanations. Lewis occasionally informs us in the journals that he has not taken exercise for some time. Is this because he has been incapacitated by dark moods? Possibly — but there may be other rational explanations. We must not view all of Lewis's behavior through the lens of his suicide.

Alexander Wilson (1776- 1813), who painted the birds brought to him in Philadelphia by Meriwether Lewis, heard of Lewis's death on November 10, 1809. He traveled all the way from Philadelphia to Tennessee to the scene of his friend's demise, wept for Lewis, and wrote this poem:

The anguish that his soul assailed,
The dark despair that round him blew,
No eye, save that of Heaven beheld,
None but unfeeling strangers knew.

Poor reason perished in the storm
And desperation triumped here!

For hence be each accusing thought,
With him my kindred tears shall flow,
Pale Pity consecrate the spot
Where poor lost Lewis now lies low.

Love as these solitudes appear
Wide as this wilderness is spread,
Affection's steps shall linger here,
To breathe her sorrows o'er the dead.[77]

Although the evidence points to melancholia, alcoholism, and suicide — after all, these are Jefferson's conclusions about a "beloved man" and protégé — I believe that the Lewis and Clark community has jumped on the bandwagon of these descriptors too uncritically, that we ought at least to maintain a healthy skepticism on so delicate a subject, and that Lewis deserves more benefit of the doubt than he tends these days to receive. One of Jefferson's three intellectual heroes, Francis Bacon, wrote, "In general, let every student of nature take this as a rule, that whatever his mind seizes and dwells upon with particular satisfaction is to be held in suspicion." It should give us pause to realize that the manic depressive Lewis is a product of "Prozac Nation." Above all, I believe that we all need to be more cautious on the question of Lewis's silences. It seems to me virtually certain that we do not now possess all that Lewis wrote in the course of the Expedition. Under any analysis, Lewis's silences were considerable and — arguably — irresponsible. But they were probably not as extreme (or as frequent) as they seem and we must constantly remind ourselves that silence does not necessarily mean depression.

Having said all of that, I do believe that the evidence supports Jefferson's conclusion that Meriwether Lewis "had from early life been subject to hypocondriac affections," and that the "sensible depressions of mind" he had observed in his secretary continued after he left the White House.[78]

One sign of Lewis's characteristic depressiveness is his willful optimism, which surfaces like a leitmotif in the journals. When he first views what he takes to be the Rocky Mountains in central Montana, he displays a pattern that characterizes his journal entries: elation, followed by a "sensible depression of spirits," followed by return to cheerfulness so resolute that he appears to protest too much.

> . . . on arriving to the summit of one of the highest points in the neighbourhood I thought myself repaid for my labour; as from this point I beheld the Rocky Mountains for the first time. . . . while I viewed these mountains I felt a secret pleasure in finding myself so near the head of the heretofore conceived boundless Missouri; but when I reflected on the difficulties which this snowey barrier would most probably throw in my way to the Pacific, and the sufferings and hardships of myself and party in them, it in some measure counterballanced the joy I had felt in the first moments in which I had gazed upon them; but as I have always held it a crime to anticipate evils I will believe it is a good, comfortable, road untill I am compelled to believe differently [May 26, 1805].

Strong language here. Why is Lewis's pleasure "secret"? Characteristically, Lewis is (or affects to be) alone. At the critical moments of the Expedition, Lewis pushes the rest of the company out of his consciousness. If he mentions a subordinate, it is usually by way of rebuke or ridicule. In his mind's eye, Lewis is always Columbus on a far shore. The phrase, "heretofore conceived boundless Missouri" points to the sense of epic heroism in Lewis's character, a pose that in the early twenty-first century smacks sometimes of Eurocentrism and bombast. At critical moments Lewis finds it impossible not to think of himself as a man of destiny. Pessimism is constantly creeping in, but he fights it with heroic will power.

The famous thirty-first birthday meditation follows the same pattern. First the gloom. My life is half over; so far I haven't done anything useful; I've wasted many hours. And then willful optimism: " . . . but since they are past and cannot be recalled, I dash from me the gloomy thought and resolved in future, to redouble my exertions. . . " [August 18, 1805].

One senses that Lewis came to identify his own worth too tightly with the prospects of the Expedition.

It is of course natural in a leader to conflate the success of his mission and his own success as a man, but one senses that Lewis came to identify his own worth too tightly with the prospects of the Expedition. Thus at the confluence of the Marias and the Missouri, Lewis declares that ascending the wrong branch " . . . would not only loose us the whole of this season but would probably so dishearten the party that it might defeat the expedition altogether" [June 3, 1805]. This is an oft-repeated refrain in Lewis's journal entries, one that William Clark never feels the need to assert on his own behalf. Clark's refrain is "we proceeded on." Lewis is more likely to worry about what "might defeat the expedition."

Suicide

Why did Meriwether Lewis commit suicide? We can, of course, never really know. He did not leave a suicide note of any sort. Unfortunately, a critically important letter Lewis wrote to Clark sometime around September 11, 1809, a letter on which Clark based his conclusion that Lewis had committed suicide ("my reason for thinking it possible is found on the letter I received from him"), has never been found.[79] It may be idle to speculate about why anyone commits suicide. Since this will be the subject of another monograph in this series, I will provide only a summary analysis here.

This much we know. By 1809 Meriwether Lewis had a world of troubles. He was drinking heavily. He was using opium, if only in the form of laudanum, the pain killer of the privileged classes of his day. His personal finances were in terrible disarray. His official accounts as Governor of northern Louisiana were in chaos, and Mr. Madison's War Department was challenging his official expenditures. He had lost the respect of the fur aristocracy of St. Louis and his government subordinates were openly contemptuous of his leadership. He had tried a number of times to find a mate without the slightest success. He had quarreled with Jefferson's naturalist friend Benjamin Smith Barton in Philadelphia.[80] There was palpable tension in his relationship with Jefferson, his patron, his hero, his protector, his boss.

Just why he found it difficult to find a wife is unclear. Perhaps it was the bowleggedness that Peachy Gilmer had noticed in his early portrait of Lewis. Perhaps it was the fact that he preferred to sleep on the floor amidst buffalo robes and bear skins! The drinking cannot have helped. Nor the flashes of temper. Nor the bouts of melancholia. Nor the self-absorption. Speculations abound. Some have suggested that Lewis had contracted venereal disease in the West and that no woman would have him.[81] Some have argued — without evidence — that Lewis was a homosexual. If he was homosexual, he was certainly in denial. He told his friend Mahlon Dickerson, "What may be my next adventure, God knows, but on this I am determined, to get a wife." This was November 3, 1807.[82]

Above all, he was being pressed by his friend Mr. Jefferson to complete his narrative of the Expedition, and — so far as we know — he had not written a single page of that long-promised, much-awaited, geopolitically-important work.

Did anything happen "out there" to bring on Lewis's mental collapse? Writers often point to Lewis's famous birthday passage on 18 August 1805 as a clue. It is an amazing passage that certainly reveals something about Lewis's impossibly high standards for himself, his blistering self-scrutiny and his chronic melancholia.

> This day I completed my thirty first year, and conceived that I had in all human probability now existed about half the period which I am to remain in this Sublunary world. I reflected that I had as yet done but little, very little indeed, to further the hapiness of the human race, or to advance the information of the succeeding generation. I viewed with regret the many hours I have spent in indolence, and now soarly feel the want of that information which those hours would have given me had they been judiciously expended. but since they are past and cannot be recalled, I dash from me the gloomy thought and resolved in future, to redouble my exertions and at least indeavour to promote those two primary objects of human existence, by giving them the aid of that portion of talents which nature and fortune have bestoed on me; or in future, to live *for mankind*, as I have heretofore lived for *myself*.—

This passage helps explain the precariousness of Lewis's mental health, but it does not, I think, qualify as something that happened "out there." At the time Lewis wrote this he was waiting alone in a Shoshone camp in the Bitterroot Mountains, uncertain of William Clark's whereabouts or his safety, late in the traveling season, with chain upon chain of mountains between him and the Columbia River, the guest of skittish and potentially hostile Indians. He was probably also ruminating the loss of the Northwest Passage. Whatever else the Bitterroots represented, they indicated almost certainly that there could be no easy portage between navigable waters of the Missouri River and navigable waters of the Columbia.

In any event, this sort of severe self-scrutiny is characteristic of the man. In a letter to Gilbert C. Russell of April 18, 1810, Jefferson alluded to Lewis's drinking problem and wrote of "the painful reflections that would necessarily produce in a mind like his." In other words, Lewis had an enormous super-ego. He could not (like Aaron Burr, for example) shrug off failure, self-indulgence, or fecklessness. Lewis's birthday meditation is precisely the kind of thing one expects in a private diary. In the most remarkable private journal in the English language, James Boswell writes, "A man cannot know himself better than by attending to the feelings of his heart. . . . I have therefore determined to keep a daily journal in which I shall set down my various sentiments and my various conduct, which will be not only useful but very agreeable. It will give me a habit of application and improve me in expression; and knowing that I am to record my transactions will make me more careful to do well."[83] What makes Lewis's birthday reflection remarkable is not that he experienced self-doubts near the source of the "heretofore deemed endless Missouri River," but that he wrote them down in a semi-public journal. They are the stuff of private spiritual meditation, not a captain's log. Had Lewis lived to revise his journals, we can be sure that he would have excised this piece of self-revelation, or at least toned it down until it was nothing more than a commander's anxiety for the success of his mission.

The single most revealing passage of the journals is the one Meriwether Lewis wrote immediately after penning his first description of the Great Falls of the Missouri River on June 13, 1805.

> after wrighting this imperfect discription I again viewed the falls and was so much disgusted with the imperfect idea which it conveyed of the scene that I determined to draw my pen across it and begin agin, but then reflected that I could not perhaps succeed better than pening the first impressions of the mind; I wished for the pencil of Salvator Rosa or the pen of Thompson, that I might be enabled to give to the enlightened world some just idea of this truly magnifficent and sublimely grand object, which has from the commencement of time been concealed from the view of civilized man; but this was fruitless and vain. I most sincerely regreted that I had not brought a crimee obscura with me by the assistance of which even I could have hoped to have done better but alas this was also out of my reach; I therefore with the assistance of my pen only indeavoured to trace some of the stronger features of this seen by the assistance of which and my recollection aided by some able pencil I hope still to give to the world some faint idea of an object which at this moment fills me with such pleasure and astonishment, and which of it's kind I will venture to ascert is second to but one in the known world.

One seed of Meriwether Lewis's suicide, I believe, can be found in this passage. It is true that what is called the "inexpressibility topos," the idea that some experience, some event is beyond the ability of the writer, perhaps any writer, to describe, is as old as western civilization and that it is particularly common in the literature of exploration.

Even so, the fact remains that Meriwether Lewis has a problem with silences. The Great Falls of the Missouri were the sublimest thing he encountered in twenty-eight months of exploration and discovery, and he could not describe them to his satisfaction. The West was mightier than the pen — at least his pen. Why couldn't Meriwether Lewis write his narrative of the Expedition after his return to civilization in late 1806? When the switch was on he was an able and even prolific writer. The self-loathing he felt at the Great Falls in not being able to provide a "just idea of this truly magnifficent and sublimely grand object" must surely be related to the silence of the last months of his life. It wasn't that he could not write. It was rather that he could not write prose equal to his own expectations.

Expectations were high in every quarter. Jefferson was eagerly expecting Lewis's account and gently nagging him about it. The Republic of Letters was eager to hear what Lewis had to say. On August 16, 1809, Jefferson wrote, "I am very often applied to know when your work will begin to appear; and I have so long promised copies to my literary correspondents in France, that I am almost bankrupt in their eyes. I shall be very happy to receive from yourself information of your expectations on this subject."[84]

But none of these expectations could equal that of Lewis himself. He was, after all, the first to see a West "which has from the commencement of time been concealed from the view of civilized man." The "first civilized man" conceit, coupled with the demands of sublimity proved to be a fatal combination for Meriwether Lewis. After years of meditating the suicide of Meriwether Lewis, I believe that if he had been able to write his book, he would not have put a gun to his head at a lonely inn on the Natchez Trace on October 11, 1809.

It cannot have been easy to be Thomas Jefferson's friend, protégé, and employee. Above all, Jefferson had one of the most facile pens in human history. He wrote at least 22,000 letters, a myriad of plans, designs, state papers, and what today would be called monographs, in addition to an important book, *Notes on the State of Virginia*, which was, in a sense, a warm-up for Lewis's narrative account of the Voyage of Discovery. Aside from the period just after the death of his beloved wife Martha, Jefferson seems never to have had difficulty putting words to paper. His productivity was not affected by his moods. In fact, Jefferson so mastered the neoclassical stoicism that was his signature response to the world that he seems never to have experienced moods in the common sense of the term. Whatever shadow existed in Jefferson lived deep in his consciousness. The surface was all cheerfulness, activity, and seemingly effortless writing. He was an indefatigable scribbler. He was the epitome of the Enlightenment *philosophe*.

Meriwether Lewis undoubtedly aspired to be such a man. Jefferson undoubtedly assumed, in his benignly presumptuous way, that Lewis would rise to that challenge. But Lewis was no stoic and his moods were not deeply buried in his being. Jefferson's answer to emotional turmoil was kinetic mental exertion. By the end of his life, Lewis's answer was grain alcohol. Jefferson was never intoxicated in the whole course of his life.

It must have been agony to be the protégé of a man who did not understand writer's block. Even if Lewis had been able to compose his narrative, he would have had to cast his prose in the shadow of his master. How could Lewis's account of the Great Falls or the source of the Missouri be equal in grandeur to Jefferson's already famous descriptions of the Natural Bridge and the confluence of the Potomac and the Shenandoah rivers? John Adams had said that Thomas Jefferson had a "peculiar felicity of expression."[85] And Adams was thinking only of Jefferson's political and epistolary writings, not his efforts at purple prose. It would be one thing to compete with Jefferson in lucidity, but it probably seemed impossible to compete with him in the evocation of the sublime, which was, of course, precisely the arena in which Lewis needed to excel. Had Lewis been the explorer agent of John Adams, James Madison, or even George Washington, he would probably have felt less pressure in writing an account of his tour. He had the glory and the burden of being the eyes of Thomas Jefferson, who knew more than anyone else about the West, who had the largest American collection of books about Louisiana, who had already written a classic of western Americana, who wrote the finest prose in the New World, a man with an effortless pen and a serene soul.

At some point Meriwether Lewis went silent. He did not write his narrative of the Expedition. He did not reply to the letters of the President of the United States. Tarleton Bates (the brother of Lewis's lieutenant governor) spoke for everyone when he noted, "Meriwether Lewis is silent, though he promised to write weekly."[86] At some point even Jefferson became annoyed. To Secretary of War Dearborn he wrote, "It is astonishing we get not one word from him."[87] And to Lewis himself Jefferson wrote on July 17, 1808, "Since I parted with you in Albemarle in Sep. last I have never had a line from you. . . ."[88] This is the first line of a letter from a man who seldom, if ever, expressed unhappiness.

Stephen Ambrose argues that Thomas Jefferson erred in posting Lewis to St. Louis as the governor of northern Louisiana because in doing so he diverted Lewis from the preparation of his journals for publication.[89] In retrospect this would certainly seem to be true, though it quite likely that Jefferson believed that Lewis would have no trouble finding time to engage in his literary pursuits and serve as a frontier governor. Jefferson could not have foreseen that Lewis would be a disastrous governor. Indeed, his prior stints at leadership — both in the White House and as the commander of the Expedition — suggested that he would make a very good public administrator, and Jefferson was surely grooming Lewis for a political career. Jefferson had written his *Notes on the State of Virginia* with a broken wrist, while his wife was in her final illness, in the wake of his humiliating retreat from the governorship of Virginia.

Still, Ambrose's point is well taken. The book was infinitely more important than the province. Even under the best of circumstances, gubernatorial burdens would impede Lewis's writing schedule. And St. Louis was a long way from the literary capital of the United States. If it is true that Jefferson had realized during the White House period that Meriwether Lewis had a drinking problem, his ability to influence (i.e. restrain) Lewis's consumption, like Newton's gravitation, would surely lessen with distance. If, as the evidence suggests, Lewis suffered from one of the worst cases of writer's block in American history, Jefferson might have been able to assist in some way if he had maintained daily contact with Lewis: an amanuensis perhaps, or cajolery, mild rebukes, the midwifery of literary conversation, contact with other men of letters at White

House dinners, access to the future Library of Congress. Jefferson might even have helped ease Lewis's depressions. Another of his famous protégés, James Monroe, expressed gratitude that Jefferson had helped him through his own long night of the soul. "I feel," Monroe wrote, "that whatever I am at present in the opinion of others or whatever I may be in future has greatly arose from your friendship." Surely Jefferson could be counted on to give one of his "determine never to be idle" lectures. To his daughter Martha, he wrote on May 21, 1787, "A mind always employed is always happy. This is the true secret, the grand recipe for felicity. The idle are the only wretched. In a world which furnishes so many emploiments which are useful, and so many which are amusing, it is our own fault if we ever know what ennui is. . . ." Jefferson was a master of this sort of paternalistic advice.

Lewis's greatest problem may not have been separation and isolation per se, but the fact of St. Louis itself. Meriwether Lewis unlocked the Missouri River for the United States. He was the "first civilized man" to visit the Great Falls of the Missouri River, second only to Niagara in sublimity. He was the "first civilized man" to bestride the source of the "heretofore deemed endless Missouri River." Endless! He was the first American to cross the entire continent. The West was the future of human liberty and Meriwether Lewis was the key that had opened it.

It was *his* Expedition. The Missouri was, in some sense, *his* river. The territory was, in some sense, *his* Louisiana. And now, having triumphed in the role of the American Columbus, he was consigned to a desk job, and not just a desk job, but a desk perched at the gateway to *his* continental wilderness. He had named the West! He knew, of course, that other men would ascend the Missouri River to take advantage of its economic treasures. He even welcomed this, promoted it in his first post-expeditionary letter to the President: "If the government will only aid, even in a very limited manner, the enterprize of her Citizens, I am fully convinced that we shal shortly derive the benifits of a most lucrative trade from this source. . . ."[90] But Meriwether Lewis was a proud man, a hyper-serious man, a romantic, and a man of destiny. He might have been able to abstract himself somewhat from the juggernaut he unleashed if he had not had to witness it at such close quarters. If he had been stationed in Louisville, or Pittsburgh or Washington, D.C., he might have been able to live down the experience — and dine out on it meanwhile.

But it cannot have been easy to sit at a desk in St. Louis and look out on America's greatest river — *his* river — and witness the antlike scurrying of other men as they prepared to ascend the great river. He did not, perhaps, wish to revisit the source himself ("what may be my next adventure, God knows"),[91] but it may be that he could not but resent the fact that other men — lesser men — were venturing on his river. They were forcing their way against the current not to map it or survey it or enumerate its wonders. They were ascending the Missouri to strip it of resources as unceremoniously as possible. They were not harbingers of Enlightenment. They were not emissaries of America's philosopher-prince. They were not scientists. They were not diplomats determined to craft respectful relations with aborginal people. They were mute inglorious Hamiltonians bent on gain. The Great Barbecue of the Nineteenth Century was about to begin.

I hasten to confess that there is not a shred of evidence in the writings of Meriwether Lewis or in statements made about him by his friends and enemies, to substantiate this claim, that he felt proprietary about the wilderness he had opened. It is, therefore, according to the principles of good history, purely speculative and illegitimate. I advance it as a suspicion only and not the sort of historical analysis that can be buttressed by textual evidence.

But this is an essay, not standard history, and it is, moreover, a humanities essay. The imperative of the humanities is to try to make sense of the life and achievement, the failure and death of Meriwether Lewis. As usual with the humanities, the facts are clear but the meaning is shrouded in mystery. I would rather work from solid evidence, of course, but in the absence of such evidence I feel the need to bring my best speculative analysis to the question, knowing that readers will simply dismiss what they do not find persuasive and that nobody will be unaware that I am now wrestling with meaning — the way we read a poem — rather than merely articulating the facts of Lewis's biography.

For too long the story of Lewis and Clark has been left to the lore aficionados. The Voyage of Discovery has been seen as a congeries of boats, guns, knives, trinkets, and campsites. Obviously, the Lewis and Clark story is in part equipage, but this is — to my mind — the least interesting part of the story.

My speculations are not the work of the library. I have spent much of my life on the Lewis and Clark Trail in a variety of transport systems. To earn the right to talk about their adventure I hiked the entire course of the Little Missouri River, from Devil's Tower in Wyoming to the middle of North Dakota, where it debouches (glorious word) into the Missouri. It was a journey that only one other man has made on foot, so far as anyone knows, Jean Baptiste Lepage, who descended from the "Black Hills" to the Mandan Villages in Dakota just in time to hire on to the Corps of Discovery's second season of travel.[92] I didn't quite eat my own moccasins, nor did I ever receive the national hug, but I knew fatigue and debility and fear and even despair in the six weeks, 650 miles of my journey. I walked through scenes of visionary enchantment. Because of that experience, I know something about spiritual claim jumping, and I know too that that river, the heretofore deemed pointless Little Missouri, now belongs to me, not to the thousand or so ranchers who live along its meanders, not to the villagers of Alzada, Montana; Camp Crook, South Dakota; and Marmarth and Medora, North Dakota. It's my river, and I don't want anyone else making claims on it or even visiting it for that matter.

I have known melancholia. I have known writer's block. I have felt "that restlessness, that inquietude, that certain indescribable something common to old bachelors." And I have tried from reading, meditation, re-enactment, and wilderness experience to learn something about the "dark despair that round him blew."

I don't claim to have found out the heart of his mystery. Who could touch so complicated a man on the right string? Still, I have left no stone unturned in my attempts to bring intellect and imagination to the challenge of fathoming Meriwether Lewis.

And I conclude: the worst thing that could have happened to Meriwether Lewis was to have to watch other men ascend the Missouri River.

There is another ramification of Lewis's proprietary relationship with the American West. From July, 1803, to at least December of 1806, Lewis was not only the supreme commander of an exploring party that enjoyed the support of the Congress, the War Department, and the President of the United States, but he was, for long stretches of time, alone in the wilderness. He was a complete sovereign in an immense landscape where he considered no man his equal, not even his friend William Clark. When he issued orders, they were immediately obeyed. In Louisiana he was operating in a military hierarchy; no political persuasion was necessary. Beyond the grid he answered to no man and he was, for a very long period of time, the most interesting and important man in the world through which he traveled.

Then came re-entry. Surely to walk into the same room as Thomas Jefferson was to be made aware instantly of subordination, no matter how magnanimous the President might be. Jefferson was the smartest, best educated, best read, best mannered man of his age, and he clung to his pet notions tenaciously. His adoring daughter, Martha, managed enough irony to declare, "My father never gave up a friend or an opinion." It cannot have been easy to be the protégé of Thomas Jefferson. And if it was difficult in the apprenticeship period of 1801-1803, it must have been impossible in the triumphal period of 1806-07.

Then there was the problem of women. In South Dakota, Meriwether Lewis had big medicine (though not perhaps so much as the Negro York). Sioux chiefs offered comely tawny damsels, and were offended by Lewis's self-restraint. It is not clear just how many women Lewis might have possessed between St. Louis and the Pacific Ocean, but the number is surely large. He might even like James T. Kirk have considered it his patriotic duty.

Then came re-entry. No civilized woman would have Meriwether Lewis. In Virginia and Pennsylvania he was as desperate to possess them as he was to resist them on the Great Plains. One even left town to avoid him. The medicine was gone. Why was his charisma greater among "savages" than among civilized women?

In civilization, there were government bureaucrats, mere clerks, who had never encountered a grizzled bear, who had never known the sublime, who had never eaten dog, but who had it in their power to plague Meriwether Lewis. Who was this State Department functionary R.S. Smith who would write, in August 1809, "The bill mentioned in this Letter having been drawn without authority it cannot be paid at this Dept." How can a desk clerk in Washington, D.C., veto the action of a sovereign governor in a faraway territory?

And then there was St. Louis, where the fur aristocrats were corruptionists and venal, wholly unimpressed by the rule of law and Thomas Jefferson's *pax Americana*, looking upon the new Governor as a potential friend to their monopolistic schemes, more likely as a pedantic obstruction to their dreams of wealth beyond the dreams of avarice, a tedious exemplar of due process and contract. And in St. Louis, Lewis's subordinate, his secretary Frederick Bates, steadfastly refused to play the subordinate. If there is an Iago in this tragedy, a subaltern whose mix of envy, contempt, vaulting ambition, and the feeling of "wounded merit," combined to prey upon the fatal weaknesses (anger, drink, delay) of a much greater man, it was Frederick Bates.

In Louisiana, Lewis carried a universal letter of credit. In St. Louis Lewis's credit proved to be hollow. In Louisiana, Lewis answered to no one. In St. Louis no one seemed to feel the need to answer to the Governor. In St. Louis, Lewis was Governor — and he faced a world of troubles. In Dakota he was a mere Captain — and his authority was unlimited. For all of his venom, Bates had it right when he concluded of Lewis, "His habits are altogether military & he never can I think succeed in any other profession."

There is also what might be called the "Buzz Aldrin syndrome." Edwin E. (Buzz) Aldrin was the second man on the moon. He first stepped on the surface of the moon a few minutes after 11:00 p.m. EDT on July 20, 1969, not long after Neil Armstrong's footfall at 10:56 p.m. Those precious minutes of primacy meant that Neil Armstrong would always be "the first man on the moon," Aldrin a frequently ignored runner-up. Aldrin was thirty-nine years old. He splashed down at 12:50 p.m. on July 24, 1969. Almost immediately, his life began to come undone. In a remarkable book, *Return to Earth*, Aldrin chronicles the sad aftermath of his journey. He used to find himself alone out by the back fence at astronaut parties in Houston looking up at the moon and asking himself, "did I ever even really go there?" He had a nervous breakdown. He took to drink. He left his wife. He became an evangelical Christian. He wondered:

When you've been to the moon, what's left?

Indeed. What do you do when you crest at thirty-nine, when the peak experience of your life is over and you have two score years more to live? You are not going back to the moon. You are not going on to Mars. How do you come down from the summit? You do not wish to sell spark plugs. The Buzz Aldrin syndrome is shared by some who return from war, by Olympic athletes, by those who engage in extreme sports, by mountain climbers, by rock stars, movie stars, child stars, and celebrities of all sorts.

Meriwether Lewis peaked early. He was thirty-two years old when he arrived at the White House, a national hero, in December of 1806. He had accomplished what no European man had ever done. He had gone where no white man had gone before. He had explored the West as Thomas Jefferson's personal emissary — but the President was not quite so enthusiastic now, on this side of the Expedition, as he had been in those yeasty early months when there were longitudinal lessons on the White House lawn, when he had thrown open his private library to his young secretary, when the news of the Louisiana Purchase was hailed as a miracle in statecraft.

When you have been to the source of the "heretofore deemed endless Missouri River," and getting there was a darling project of most of your life, what's left? A few prosecutorial tasks in the Burr conspiracy crisis? Endless paperwork? The attempt to manage a pack of wicked, venal, corrupt, anti-republican fur acquisitives like Manuel Lisa? Vouchers?

In the course of his twenty-eight-month tour, Lewis looked into the mirror countless times. There are two kinds of people in the world, those who can look in the mirror and maintain their identity and self-regard, and those whose essential view of themselves is disintegrated by that experience. William Clark remained intact. Meriwether Lewis came undone. It is perhaps true that Clark had fewer opportunities to gaze into the mirror than did Meriwether Lewis, given the division of duties they established early in the Voyage of Discovery. But it is also the case that Lewis was — like the golden boy Narcissus — more disposed to look in the mirror than was Clark. Clark's journal entries are remarkable for their earthy candor, their clarity, their unpretentiousness. But there is scarcely a reflective sentence in all of his voluminous prose. It does not simplify the record to assert that Lewis was the expedition's philosopher, Clark its primary reporter. Meriwether Lewis had a more sensitive and complicated soul than his partner in discovery.

Meriwether Lewis was the kind of man who is disposed to self-examination. By the time he embarked on his famous journey into the heart of the American wilderness, Lewis was already a man whose ego-identity structure was fragile. The events of the Expedition did not break his spirit, but they had the cumulative effect of weakening his psychological immune system. By the time he returned to the White House he was emotionally exhausted. When the real crisis came in 1808 and 1809 there was no soul reserve to draw on. A wife might have helped. A rooted home might have made the difference — think of the psychic transfusions Thomas Jefferson took from his beloved Monticello in the course of his crisis-ridden life. A Presidential friend in proximity might have helped. Surely William Clark did what he could to help, but by now he was floating down the stream of his life while Lewis continued to explore the upper tributaries of his. Lewis's encounters with the Other, with "scenes of visionary enchantment," with "tawny damsels" and "capricious Indians," the "national hug" and "imps of satturn," with hunger, cold, fear, bewilderment, the strain of leadership, formidable and sometimes hostile quadrupeds, seem to have weakened his self-confidence.

It might have been otherwise. He might have come back from the West a conquering hero, like Odysseus, and set his house in order. Instead, his post-Expedition course of self-destruction could scarcely have been more rapid or deliberate. Drugs, alcohol, broken relationships, disturbed friendships, quarrels public and private, and terminal writer's block carried Meriwether Lewis to his death in a miserable hut in Tennessee. What a falling off was there. He wouldn't even try the bed.

It is foolhardy to try to reduce a great man's suicide to a single cause. Meriwether Lewis did not leave a suicide note. We know that he was raging about the War Department in the last hours of his life, and his "enemies," but our sources are unreliable and that surely is only part of the story. In his last hours of delusion he announced to those around him that Clark was just behind, coming as always to set things right. It is true that Clark was on his way to Washington, D.C. in October of 1809, but he had never intended to follow the trail of his mercurial friend. He was hundreds of miles away at the time of the fatal shooting.

Still, if I were pressed to name a "cause" of Lewis's suicide, I would jump over drink and love's labor's lost and writer's block and War Department vouchers, and say, one too many mirrors.

One of the first newspapers to report Lewis's suicide, the *Democratic Clarion* of Nashville, Tennessee, wrote a fitting epitaph: "In the death of Governor Lewis, the public behold the wreck of one of the noblest men."

Some men don't belong in the wilderness: Charbonneau. Some don't belong in civilization: John Colter. And a few, having spent time in both, find they no longer have a home in either world.

> *"In the death of Governor Lewis, the public behold the wreck of one of the noblest men. He was a pupil of the immortal Jefferson, by him he was reared, by him he was instructed in the tour of the sciences, by him he was introduced to public life when his enterprizing soul, great botanical knowledge, acute penetration and personal courage soon pointed him out as the most proper person to command a projected exploring party to the Northwest Coast of the American Continent."*
>
> —*Democratic Clarion* (Nashville), October 20, 1809[93]

Endnotes

1. "Jefferson to Benjamin Smith Barton, Feb. 27. 1803," in Donald Jackson, ed., *Letters of the Lewis and Clark Expedition with Related Documents, 1783-1854* (Urbana: University of Illinois Press, 1978), vol I, pp. 16-17.

2. Albert Furtwangler, *Acts of Discovery: Visions of America in the Lewis and Clark Journals* (Urbana: University of Illinois Press, 1993), p, 159.

3. Quoted in *Boswell's Life of Johnson*, Frank Brady, ed. (New York: The New American Library, 1968), p. 32.

4. Quoted in Stephen Ambrose, *Undaunted Courage: Meriwether Lewis, Thomas Jefferson and the Opening of the American West* (New York: Simon & Shuster, 1996), p. 27.

5. Ambrose, p. 464.

6. Ambrose, p. 417.

7. Letter from Thomas Jefferson to Benjamin Austin, January 9, 1816: "He, therefore, who is now against domestic manufacture, must be for reducing us either to dependence on that foreign nation, or to be clothed in skins, and to live like wild beasts in dens and caverns. I am not one of these."

8. Quoted in Richard Dillon, *Meriwether Lewis: A Biography* (New York: Coward-McCann, 1965), p. 23.

9. Dillon, p. 87.

10. Ambrose, p. 435.

11. Dillon, p. 262.

12. The president's abode was not called the White House until after the War of 1812. I use the term as shorthand.

13. Marie Goegel Kimball, *Thomas Jefferson's Cookbook* (Charlottesville, Virginia: University Press of Virginia), p. 18.

14. Quoted in Kimball, vii.

15. "There's no accounting for taste."

16. George Drouillard (?-1810) was arguably the third most important member of the Expedition. The captains pronounced and spelled his name Drewyer. Meriwether Lewis recruited him at Fort Massac (in today's Illinois) in November 1803.

17. Clark calls the steelhead trout a "*Salmon trout*," and reports that it was "fried in a little Bears oil which a Chief gave us yesterday. . . ."

18. Attributed to Otto von Bismarck.

19. Furtwangler, p. 95.

20. Quoted in Paul Russell Cutright, *Lewis & Clark: Pioneering Naturalists* (Lincoln and London: University of Nebraska Press, 1989), pp. 383-384.

21. Furtwangler, p. 148.

22. Furtwangler p. 149.

23. Jefferson to Benjamin Rush, February 28, 1803, quoted in Jackson, vol. I, p. 18.

24. Lewis to Lucy Marks, March 31, 1805, quoted in Jackson, vol. I, p. 225.

25. The Lewis and Clark Expedition was a transcontinental journey. Although May 14, 1804 is usually listed as the starting date for the Expedition, the fact is that Lewis began his descent of the Ohio River on August 31, 1803 in the keelboat which eventually made its way all the way from Pittsburgh to the Mandan villages in what is now North Dakota. Lewis began keeping a formal journal at the beginning of the Ohio adventure on August 31, 1803, and not on May 14, 1804. His last entry was on August 12, 1806, when he declares that he is suspending his journal because of the gunshot wound he suffered at the hands of Pierre Cruzatte. Moulton includes journal entries by Meriwether Lewis for 418 of the 1120 days from August 31, 1803 through September 23, 1806, including August 31 (Lewis entered the date incorrectly as August 30) to September 18, 1805 (19 days); November 11 to November 28, 1803 (18 days); May 14 (probable, not dated), 15, 20, 1804 (3 days); September 16-17, 1804 (2 days); April 7 to August 26, 1805 (142 days); September 9-10 and 18-22, November 29-December 1, 1805 (10 days); January 1 to August 12, 1806 (224 days). This list of does not account for official expeditionary orders, field notes, and court-martial proceedings, some of which were probably written by Meriwether Lewis.

26. Ambrose, p. 167.

27. *Cap-à-pie*, "armed from head to foot."

28. Gary E. Moulton, editor, *The Journals of the Lewis & Clark Expedition* (Lincoln and London: University of Nebraska Press, 1990), vol. 6, p. 157.

29. Jefferson to John Minor, August 30, 1814.

30. Quoted in Ambrose, p. 41.

31. Quoted in Ambrose, p. 42.

32. Rhys Carpenter, *Folktale, Fiction and Saga in the Homeric Epics* (Berkeley, California: University of California Press, 1962).

33. Tocqueville says in "Influence of Mores upon the Maintenance of a Democratic Republic in the United States that ". . . I consider mores to be one of the great general causes responsible for maintenance of a democratic republic in the United States. I here mean the term 'mores' (*moeurs*) to have its original Latin meaning; I mean it to apply not only to "*moeurs*" in the strict sense, which might be called the habits of the heart, but also to the different notions possessed by men, the various opinions current among them, and the sum of ideas that shape mental habits." Alexis de Tocqueville, *Democracy in America*, translated by George Lawrence, edited by J.P. Mayer (New York: Harper & Row Perennial Library edition, 1988), p. 287.

34. Lewis to Clark, May 29, 1808, quoted in Ambrose, p. 448.

35. Actually, on May 25, 1805, Clark consulted an encyclopedia that was part of the Expedition's traveling library. He referred to it as a "Deckinsery of arts and ciences."

36. Jackson, vol. II, p. 720.

37. Lewis to Mahlon Dickerson, November 3, 1807.

38. Elliot Coues, editor, *The History of the Lewis and Clark Expedition* (New York: Dover Publications, Inc.), vol. 1, pp. 221-222.

39. Quoted in Ambrose, p. 476.

40. Quoted in Ambrose, p. 209.

41. Quoted in Ambrose, pp. 59-60.

42. Heraclitus (535-475 BCE) was the pre-socratic Greek philosopher who argued that the world was in a state of unending flux: "You cannot step twice into the same river."

43. Jefferson to Paul Allen, August 18, 1813, quoted in Jackson, vol. II, p. 589.

44. Opinions vary about the "source" of the Missouri River. The headwaters are, of course, formed by the joining of the Madison, Gallatin, and Jefferson rivers. Lewis followed the Jefferson to present-day Beaverhead River, where Red Rock River and Horse Prairie Creek join. Lewis considered Horse Prairie Creek the ultimate headwater of the Missouri. Modern geographers say that it is Red Rock River, which originates near the Continental Divide and Yellowstone National Park. If this is true, Thomas Jefferson's search for a height of land where the great western rivers interlock is not so absurd.

45. See missing dates on page 30. See also note 25, page 118.

46. Lewis to Jefferson, April 7, 1805, quoted in Donald Jackson I, p. 232.

47. David McKeehan to Lewis, April 7, 1807, quoted in Jackson, vol. II, p. 401.

48. Lewis to Jefferson, September 8, 1803, quoted in Jackson, vol. I, pp. 121-122.

49. Quoted in Dillon, p. 97.

50. Jefferson to Thomas Jefferson Randolph, November 24, 1808: "In truth, politeness is artificial good humor, it covers the natural want of it, and ends by rendering habitual a substitute nearly equivalent to the real virtue. It is the practice of sacrificing to those whom we meet in society all the little conveniences and preferences which will gratify them, and deprive us of nothing worth a moment's consideration; it is the giving a pleasing and flattering turn to our expressions which will conciliate others, and make them pleased with us as well as themselves. How cheap a price for the good will of another!"

51. Quoted in Dillon, p. 97.

52. Quoted in Dillon. p. 143.

53. Quoted in Moulton, vol. III, p. 418.

54. Jefferson to Lewis, January 22, 1804, quoted in Jackson, vol. 1, p. 166.

55. Jackson, vol. II, p. 385.

56. Jackson, vol. II, p. 405.

57. Ambrose, p. 25.

58. Ambrose, p. 42.

59. Ambrose, p. 45.

60. Quoted in Dillon, p. 341.

61. To Charles Bellini, September 30, 1785: "Here [France], it seems that a man might pass a life without encountering a single rudeness. In the pleasures of the table, they are far before us, because, with good taste they unite temperance. They do not terminate the most sociable meals by transforming themselves into brutes. I have never yet seen a man drunk in France, even among the lowest of the people."

62. Quoted in Dillion, p. 308.

63. Levi Lincoln to Jefferson, April 17, 1803, quoted in Jackson, vol. 1, p. 35.

64. "Jefferson's Instructions to Lewis," quoted in Jackson, vol. 1, pp. 61-65.

65. *The Odyssey of Homer*, translated by Richmond Lattimore book ix, lines 407ff.

66. *The Odyssey of Homer,* book ix, lines 502-505.

67. Jefferson to Vine Utley, March 21, 1819.

68. Samuel Taylor Coleridge, *Biographia Literaria*, 1817.

69. *King Lear*, act III, scene iv.

70. *Hamlet,* act IV, scene iv.

71. *The Tempest*, act V, scene i.

72. Jefferson to the Wolf and people of the Mandan nation, December 30, 1806.

73. Quoted in M.R. Montgomery, *Jefferson and the Gun-Men: How the West Was Almost Lost* (New York: Crown Publishers, 2000), pp. 164-165.

74. Jackson, vol. I, p. 315.

75. Quoted in Dillon, p. 15.

76. From a poem by Alexander Wilson, quoted in Dillon, p. 340.

77. See Note 76.

78. Jefferson to Paul Allen, August 18, 1813, quoted in Jackson, vol. II, pp. 591-592.

79. Ambrose, p. 476.

80. Dillon, p. 342.

81. Reimert Thorolf Ravenholt, "Triumph Then Despair: The Tragic Death of Meriwether Lewis." *Epidemiology*, vol. 5, number 3 (May 1994), pp. 366-79.

82. Quoted in Dillon, p. 285.

83. *Boswell's London Journal: 1762-1763*, ed. Frederick A. Pottle, p. 39.

84. Quoted in Jackson, vol. 1, p. 458-459.

85. John Adams in a letter to Timothy Pickering, August 6, 1822, responding to a question about the writing of the Declaration of Independence, writes, "Mr. Jefferson came into Congress in June, 1775, and brought with him a reputation for literature, science, and a happy talent of composition. Writings of his were handed about, remarkable for the peculiar felicity of expression."

86. Quoted in Dillon, p. 307.

87. Jackson, vol. II, p. 445n. Jefferson to Dearborn, August 12, 1808.

88. Jackson, vol. II, p. 444.

89. "This was a big mistake, easily avoidable. Jefferson would have done much better to promote Lewis to higher rank and assign him to duty in the War Department with no other responsibility than working with secretarial help and special advisers in getting the journals published promptly by the government." Ambrose, p. 417.

90. Quoted in Jackson, vol. I., p. 322.

91. Lewis to Mahlon Dickerson, quoted in Dillon, p. 285.

92. Moulton, III., p. 227.

93. Quoted in Dillon, p. 335.

A Concise Meriwether Lewis Reading List

Abrams, Rochonne. "The Colonial Childhood of Meriwether Lewis." *Bulletin of the Missouri Historical Society*, vol. xxiv (July 1978).

Allen, John Logan. *Passage through the Garden: Lewis and Clark and the Image of the American Northwest*. Urbana: University of Illinois Press, 1975.

Ambrose, Stephen. *Undaunted Courage: Meriwether Lewis, Thomas Jefferson, and the Opening of the American West*. New York: Simon & Schuster, 1996.

Appelman, Roy. *Lewis and Clark*. Washington, D.C.: National Park Service, 1975.

Bakeless, John. *Lewis and Clark: Partners in Discovery*. New York: William Morrow, 1947.

Chuinard, Eldon G. "The Court Martial of Ensign Meriwether Lewis." *We Proceeded On*, vol. 8, no. 4 (November, 1982).

Criswell, Elijan H. *Lewis and Clark: Linguistic Pioneers*. Columbia, MO: University of Missouri Press, 1940.

Cutright, Paul Russell. "Meriwether Lewis's 'Coloring of Events.'" *We Proceeded On*, vol. 11, no. 1 (February 1985).

Cutright. "The Journal of Captain Meriwether Lewis." *We Proceeded On*, vol. 10, no. 1 (February 1984).

Cutright. *A History of the Lewis and Clark Journals*. Norman: University of Oklahoma Press, 1976.

Cutright. "Rest, Rest, Perturbed Spirit." *We Proceeded On*, vol. 12, no. 1 (March 1986).

Dillon, Richard. *Meriwether Lewis: A Biography*. New York: Coward-McCann, 1965.

Fisher, Vardis. *Suicide or Murder? The Strange Death of Governor Meriwether Lewis*. Chicago: Swallow Press, 1962.

Furtwangler, Albert. *Acts of Discovery: Visions of America in the Lewis and Clark Journals*. Urbana: University of Illinois Press, 1993.

Jackson, Donald, ed. *The Letters of the Lewis and Clark Expedition, with Related Documents: 1783-1854*. 2nd ed. Urbana: University of Illinois Press, 1978.

Jackson. "Jefferson, Meriwether Lewis, and the Reduction of the United States Army." *Proceedings of the American Philosophical Society*, vol. 124, no. 2 (April, 1980).

Montgomery, M.R. *Jefferson and the Gun-Men: How the West Was Almost Lost*. New York: Crown Publishers , 2000.

Moulton, Gary. *The Journals of the Lewis & Clark Expedition*. Lincoln: University of Nebraska Press, 1988.

Phelps, Dawson A. "The Tragic Death of Meriwether Lewis." *William and Mary Quarterly*, vol. XIII, no. 3 (1956).

Ravenholt, Reimert Thorolf. "Triumph Then Despair: The Tragic Death of Meriwether Lewis." *Epidemiology*, vol. 5, no. 3 (May 1994).

Ronda, James. *Lewis and Clark Among the Indians*. Lincoln: University of Nebraska Press, 1984.

Sheehan, Bernard W. *Seeds of Extinction: Jeffersonian Philanthropy and the American Indian*. Chapel Hill: University of North Carolina Press, 1973.

Wallace, Anthony F.C. *Jefferson and the Indians: The Tragic Fate of the First Americans*. Cambridge: The Belknap Press of Harvard University Press, 1999.

Members of the Expedition

***Meriwether Lewis** (1774-1809) ***William Clark** (1770-1838)

Sergeants

Charles Floyd (1782-1804)
(died of ruptured appendix)

***Patrick Gass** (1771-1870)
(elected Sergeant to replace Floyd)

***John Ordway** (ca. 1775-ca. 1817)

***Nathaniel Pryor** (1772-1831)

Corporal Richard Warfington (1777-?) was in charge of a group of men who returned to St. Louis in April 1805 with the keelboat. Others returned in June 1804. Those who left St. Louis include Privates John Boley, John Dame, Ebenezer Tuttle, John Robertson, and Issac White, as well as several nonmilitary *engagés* (French-speaking boatmen), one of whom deserted.

Privates

***William E. Bratton** (1778-1841)

***John Collins** (?-1823)

***John Colter** (ca. 1775-1813)

***Pierre Cruzatte** (dates unknown)

***Joseph Field** (ca. 1772-1807)

***Reubin Field** (ca. 1771-1823?)

***Robert Frazer** (?-1837)

***George Gibson** (?-1809)

***Silas Goodrich** (dates unknown)

***Hugh Hall** (ca. 1772-?)

***Thomas P. Howard** (1779-?)

***François Labiche** (dates unknown)

***Jean Baptiste Lepage**
(unknown dates, *replaced Newman at Fort Mandan*)

***Hugh McNeal** (dates unknown)

John Newman (ca. 1785-1838)
(expelled, returned in 1805)

***John Potts** (1776-1808)

Moses Reed (dates unknown)
(expelled, returned in 1805)

***George Shannon** (1785-1836)

***John Shields** (1769-1809)

***John B. Thompson**
(dates unknown)

***Peter M. Weiser** (1781-?)

***William Werner** (dates unknown)

***Joseph Whitehouse** (ca. 1775-?)

***Alexander Willard** (1778-1865)

***Richard Windsor** (dates unknown)

Others

***Toussaint Charbonneau**
(about 1758-before 1843)
(hired as an interpreter at Fort Mandan)

***Jean Baptiste "Pomp" Charbonneau**(1805-1866)
(son of Charbonneau & Sacagawea)

***George Drouillard** (?-1810)
(hired as an interpreter, name usually spelled "Drewyer")

***Sacagawea** (about 1788-90 to 1812)
(Shoshone, wife of Charbonneau, gave birth to son at Fort Mandan after Charbonneau joined the Expedition)

***Seaman (aka Scannon)**
(Lewis's Newfoundland dog)

***York** (ca. 1770-?)
(Clark's slave, companion from childhood)

Members who traveled from Fort Mandan to Fort Clatsop and returned — 33 humans and Seaman the dog, are marked with an asterisk (*). Those who kept journals include Gass, Floyd, Frazer, Ordway, and Whitehouse If Sergeant Pryor kept one, it has been lost, as has the journal of Private Frazer, who received permission to publish. The youngest member of the Expedition, George Shannon, assisted Nicholas Biddle in preparing the first edition of the journals for publication.

The Marmarth Institute

Marmarth is a near-ghost town on the Little Missouri River in southwestern North Dakota. Clay Jenkinson's dream is to create a Great Plains think tank in Marmarth, a retreat center for artists, writers, meditatives, saunterers, and others who feel the need to spend some time beyond the grid. The Marmarth Institute hosts seminars, residencies, symposiums, and retreats in one of the most beautiful and improbable places in North America. Participants can hike, canoe, kayak, camp, milk goats, fast, perform sweat lodge ceremonies, read, make cheese, fix fence, study the stars, dig for dinosaur bones, ride horses, keep journals, paint, meditate, or just plain talk.

A portion of all Marmarth Press profits benefits the Marmarth Institute.

The Marmarth Institute consists of four buildings: the historically significant Barber Auditorium, an abandoned brick bank building, a former Milwaukee Road depot and bunkhouse, and the Mystic Theater, which is on the National Registry of Historic Buildings. All of these buildings lie on the two main streets of Marmarth, near the North Dakota, South Dakota, Montana border.

The Marmarth Institute exists to promote the agrarian dream of Thomas Jefferson, to study sustainability questions, to promote the ideals of the Enlightenment, and to envision a time when First World humans learn to live more lightly on the planet.

For more information visit our website at www.th-jefferson.org or contact the local custodian of the Marmarth Institute, Patti Perry, at 701-279-6996.

About Clay S. Jenkinson

Clay Jenkinson is a North Dakotan. He grew up between the watersheds of the Little Missouri and Missouri rivers. He spent summers on a dairy farm in Minnesota. He holds degrees from the University of Minnesota and Oxford University, where he was a Rhodes and Danforth Scholar. He has taught at Pomona College, the University of Colorado, the law school of the University of North Dakota, and at the University of Nevada at Reno.

Clay Jenkinson has driven the Lewis and Clark Trail half a dozen times, hiked and canoed and kayaked whole swaths of it, camped where Lewis and Clark camped, and lounged on the last sandbars of the Missouri River. In 1985 he hiked the entire course of the Little Missouri River from Devil's Tower in Wyoming to its confluence with the Missouri in western North Dakota. He spent the Millennium alone on Bullion Butte in western North Dakota with the wind chill at -100°. He is the only Lewis and Clark scholar who has flown over the oxbows of the Missouri River in an F-16 fighter jet.

Although Clay Jenkinson was trained in the classics and English Renaissance Literature, he is now primarily known as a Thomas Jefferson scholar. His book, *The Paradox of Thomas Jeffer-*

son, will soon be published. He has lectured widely on the life and achievement of Thomas Jefferson, including at Monticello, and his award-winning portrayals of the Third President have won universal respect. Clay Jenkinson has also portrayed Meriwether Lewis throughout the United States.

Clay Jenkinson is a Senior Fellow with the Center for Digital Government in Sacramento, California, the co-founder of the Great Plains Chautauqua, the director of the Great Basin Chautauqua, a member of the American Antiquarian Society, and the Custodian of the Marmarth Institute.

Clay Jenkinson currently lives in Reno, Nevada, with his daughter Catherine Missouri. He is the creator and host of the nationally-syndicated public radio program "The Thomas Jefferson Hour."

Clay Jenkinson was the principal on-air consultant in Ken Burns' 1997 documentary study of *Thomas Jefferson*, a consultant to Burns' *Lewis and Clark*, and the host, scriptwriter, and principal consultant for Freewheelin' Films' *Travelin' On: The Lewis and Clark Trail*.

Index

Page number followed by an "n" in italics and another number refer to an endnote found on that page. Members of the Expedition are marked with an asterisk (*) and are listed on page 124.